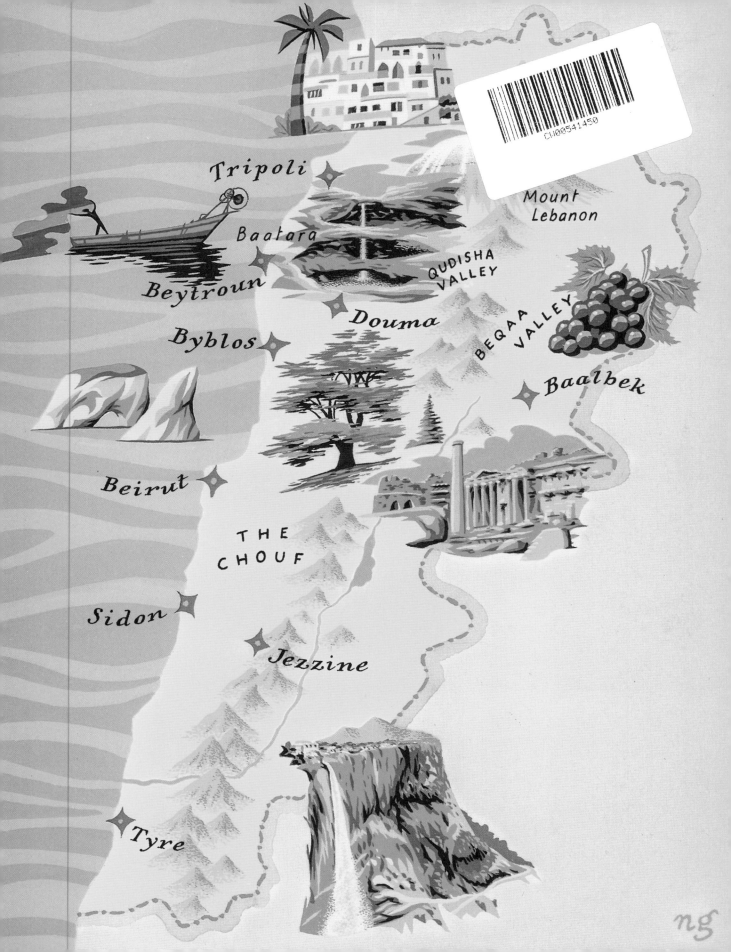

SAFFRON
IN THE
SOUKS

زعفران في السوق

John Gregory-Smith is a best-selling author, presenter and food and travel writer who specialises in Middle Eastern and North African cuisine. He has published four books, including *Orange Blossom & Honey*, *Turkish Delights*, *Mighty Spice Express* and *The Mighty Spice Cookbook*. John appears regularly on Channel 4's Sunday Brunch and has recently written for *Condé Nast Traveller*, *Delicious Magazine*, *British Airways High Life*, *Grazia*, *Olive Magazine*, *Out There*, *Evening Standard* and *Sainsbury's Magazine*.

SAFFRON
IN THE
SOUKS

VIBRANT RECIPES FROM
THE HEART OF LEBANON

JOHN GREGORY-SMITH

Food photography by Nassima Rothacker
Location photography by Alan Keohane

KYLE BOOKS

To Kamal Mouzawak, for unlocking the land for me.

An Hachette UK Company
www.hachette.co.uk

First published in Great Britain in 2019 by
Kyle Books, an imprint of Kyle Cathie Ltd
Carmelite House
50 Victoria Embankment
London EC4Y 0DZ
www.kylebooks.co.uk

ISBN: 9780857835772

Publisher: Joanna Copestick
Editor: Tara O'Sullivan
Design: Smith & Gilmour
Food photography: Nassima Rothacker
Location photography: Alan Keohane
Food stylist: Rosie Reynolds
Props stylist: Wei Tang
Map artwork: Neil Gower

A Cataloguing in Publication record for this title is available from the British Library.

Printed and bound in China

10 9 8 7 6 5 4 3 2 1

CONTENTS

DISCOVERING LEBANON

When I was writing my first cookbook back in 2010, I went to work as a chef in a restaurant in Beirut called Souk El Tayeb. The owner, Kamal Mouzawak, had set up a space where he could invite women from different regions of Lebanon to come and share their home-cooked recipes with a wider audience. Thanks to Kamal, I worked with cooks from across the country and got to understand how unique the cuisine was. I adored the sour tang that the Lebanese palate is so partial to and the intricate use of herbs and spices, including za'atar, sumac and Lebanese 7 spice. During my time off, I explored the different neighbourhoods of Beirut and enjoyed feasting in each one. It was fascinating to be somewhere that during my childhood had always been associated with news reports about war and conflict. I got to make up my own mind about the city, its people and the food. And you know what? I was hooked.

On that first trip to Beirut, I was advised not to leave the city. I'm quite adventurous when I travel, especially if there's a whiff of a new recipe in the air, but I trust my instincts and those of the people around me. If the locals say not to do something, I won't. I went home with many fond memories, firm friends and a strong desire to return. It was the groundwork for this book. So when I decided to write *Saffron in the Souks*, I was thrilled to be told that Lebanon was now a different place. The country had settled down and it was safe for me to go and explore. I can't tell you how happy this made me. Not just for my own research, but more importantly, to think that such a beautiful part of the world was blooming again.

I set off in a battered old hire car and drove around the country from the sun-soaked souks of Saida up to Mount Lebanon and over to Beqaa Valley, the agricultural heart of the country. I marvelled at the Roman ruins in Baalbek,

picked fresh za'atar in Nabatieh and ate street food in Tripoli. I partied in Beirut, hiked through the cedar forests of Bsharri and learnt how to bake bread in a small Druze village in the Chouf Mountains. The whole time I felt completely safe and so well looked after. I experienced such generous hospitality and discovered a rich food culture. It would be foolish, however, to ignore the fact that Lebanon is in a very volatile part of the world. On a recent trip, British, American and French forces flew over the village where I was staying on a mission to bomb a chemical weapons factory near Damascus in Syria. I was only 80 kilometres from that city. Apart from a worried call from my family, I didn't notice a thing. No one around me even flinched. It just goes to show that everyone's norm is different, and when you are used to a fiery environment, 80 kilometres is a world away.

HIDDEN BEAUTY

Talking to people back home in the UK, whenever I asked what they thought about Lebanon everyone was enthusiastic about the food. People loved hummus, tabouleh, falafel and shawarma. What a great start. But when I went deeper and asked about the country itself, no one knew anything more than war. And yes, of course, this can't be overlooked; it hangs over everything. But there is so much more to Lebanon than this. It's truly beautiful, with landscapes unlike anywhere else in the world and food that's quite simply divine. That's what I want you to experience through my book, this positive side of the country that I have grown so fond of.

My first visit to Tripoli, Lebanon's second largest city, was on a rather rainy spring morning. I started off in El Mina, the oldest part of town where the Phoenicians settled some three thousand years

ago. The fish market was buzzing. Bright blue plastic tables groaned under the weight of shimmering octopuses, huge king prawns and anchovies that glistened like silver. I walked around to the harbour and ate *ashta* (clotted cream) ice cream in the rain, watching the boats bob up and down on the sea. By the afternoon the rain had cleared and the sun was scorching. I sought shade in the souk and feasted on bowls of hummus and tart pickles. I wound my way through narrow alleyways lined with piles of fresh fruits, vegetables, herbs and spices. There is quite an Arabic feel to the city; old boys were smoking shisha and drinking thick black coffee outside little cafes and the women doing their shopping were more traditionally covered than I had seen in Beirut. It all added to the essence of the city and I was utterly enchanted.

After leaving Tripoli, I went hiking around Jezzine in the Lebanese mountains. An impressive waterfall cuts through the centre of the town, spilling down into the lush valley below. I walked through thick pine forests and across meadows strewn with purple irises, pink orchids, red poppies and white geraniums. The sweet scent of wild herbs wafted up through the verdant grass. Plump cherries, soft peaches and crisp pears hung from the trees. I climbed up onto the mountaintop and sat with my legs dangling over the edge. Hazy hills strewn with pretty villages rolled all the way down to the sea. I could make out quiet squares and little stone churches in each one. This was so far from what I'd imagined I would experience, more Tuscan than Middle Eastern, and a world away from Tripoli.

I called this book *Saffron in the Souks* because, for me, the name conjures up something exciting, exotic and mysterious. It encapsulates the hidden beauty of that vibrant souk in Tripoli and the quiet calm I felt in the mountains: positive, beautiful experiences that I wanted to communicate through every element of my book.

THE LAY OF THE LAND

The history of Lebanon is deeply complex. There has been so much bloodshed over the years. I'm neither a historian nor a political writer, and when I travel to a country to understand the food, I try as best as I can to put these factors to one side. That might sound rather odd, but taking things at face value and meeting people without any preconceived ideas helps me better understand the culture, especially in parts of the world where I might not agree with political and religious practices. Despite this, the fact remains that when writing about any country, it's impossible to ignore its history and culture; after all, these aspects shape a nation's identity – and its cuisine. So here is a very brief overview – and if you want to find out more, I urge you to dive in and get researching. It's a fascinating country.

Since the third millennia, Canaanites (or, as the Greeks referred to them, Phoenicians) inhabited the region we know as Lebanon. The name Phoenicia derived from an ancient Greek word, *phoinios*, meaning purple, in reference to a dye the people were famous for extracting from a sea snail called a murex. Prized for its deep colour, the dye became the iconic purple worn by Roman emperors and their elite generals. By the ninth century BCE the Phoenicians had become one of the great trading powers of the ancient world, exporting cedar wood, olive oil, wine, dye and glass all over the Mediterranean region and even as far as the Atlantic coast of Africa. In Phoenicia they established Tyre, Sidon (Saida), Gubla (Byblos), Tripoli and Berytus (Beirut), all of which are still inhabited today.

The powerhouses of the ancient world all took control of Phoenicia. In the eighth century BCE the Assyrians ruled, followed by the Babylonians after them. In 539 BCE the Persian leader Cyrus conquered Phoenicia. Alexander the Great added the colony to his portfolio when he fought off the Persian Empire and in 64 BCE the Romans took control, connecting the country with a network of roads and building vast cities and beautiful temples along the way. In the sixth century CE a series of powerful earthquakes hit Baalbek and Beirut, which, coupled with religious disputes, weakened Rome's control. Seeing an opportunity, invaders from the Arabian Peninsula swept in and by the first half of the seventh century conquered Lebanon.

The Crusades, which lasted for more than two centuries as Christian countries attempted to take the Holy Land from Muslim rule, began in 1095 CE, the first campaign sanctioned by Pope Urban II. Although the Crusaders never established a permanent foothold in Lebanon, great castles and mighty fortresses were built all along the coast, the largest being the Citadel of Raymond de Saint-Gilles that still towers over Tripoli today. After the Crusades finally ended, fighting began between Mongol warriors from Central Asia and the Mamluk army of Egypt. The Mamluks took control of the land, eventually falling themselves to the Ottomans. During the Mamluk reign, an Egyptian known as al-Darazi settled in southern Lebanon. His followers became known as Druze, a religion based on Ismaili Islam that believes in reincarnation. They still live in Lebanon today and are famous for their incredible baking skills. It was through two powerful Druze families that the Ottomans semi-autonomously ruled Lebanon until the twentieth century when the French mandate began after World War I.

Lebanon gained its independence in 1943, and over the following decades unrest built in the country and surrounding areas, culminating in the horrendous civil war that ripped Lebanon apart for fifteen years, ending in 1990. As things began to be rebuilt, wars in neighbouring countries caused a mass influx of refugees – over thirty thousand Palestinians and almost 1.5 million Syrians are living in the country today. Lebanon has a history of taking in refugees: in 1915 Armenians fleeing genocide settled in a district in Beirut, Bourj Hammoud, which is one of my favourite parts of the city, and in Anjar in Beqaa Valley. These events have shaped the Lebanon of today, a melting pot of cultures including Muslims, Druze, Christians, Armenians, Syrians and Palestinians, all of whom have defined the cuisine.

KITCHEN CONFIDENTIAL

Lebanon has such a wide variety of exciting produce that makes its cuisine so interesting; coriander, parsley and mint are used in abundance. Garlic is lushly added to everything. Ground cherry pips (*mahlab*), rose water and orange blossom perfume decadent desserts. Kitchens will never run out of woody allspice or Lebanese 7 spice, a pungent blend made up of black peppercorns, cinnamon, ginger, cloves, nutmeg, coriander and allspice. If you can't get hold of this, use *baharat*, which is more widely available. Sumac, a beautiful crushed red berry, along with pomegranate molasses and lemon add a sour freshness to the food, a flavour the Lebanese simply adore.

Seasonal ingredients – such as spring broad beans and autumnal pomegranates – dominate dishes at the right time of the year. Vineyards producing world-class grapes flourish the length and breadth of Beqaa Valley, an area also known for producing the best lamb in the country. Olives adorn every table and nuts garnish both sweet and savoury dishes. Tahini, a paste made from ground sesame seeds, enriches everything from hummus to salads. It's also mixed with yogurt, lemon and water to make tarator sauce, which gives a decadent finish to many recipes.

In the Hezbollah-controlled south, Abu Kassem grows the finest za'atar in the world. Za'atar as we know it is a blend of sesame seeds, sumac and thyme. It is also the name of a fragrant herb that has grown wild in these lands for centuries.

The fresh herb is used to make fattoush, or is mixed with tomatoes and onions as a simple side salad. It can be dried and combined with oil or used to make the za'atar blend with sumac and sesame seeds, which is slathered onto flatbreads called *man'ouche* (see page 158). On his little farm just outside the village of Nabatieh, Abu was the first farmer to grow the crop commercially and now he supplies restaurants from Beirut to Boston. He told me that Lebanese mums tell their children to eat za'atar if they want to get smarter: a clever ruse and one that might explain why it's such a popular flavour in the country. Lebanon is not a big country, just over 10,000 square kilometres, flanked by the Mediterranean on one side and great mountains on the other. The dazzling waters off its long coastline are rich with seafood. Calamari is on every meze menu and a dish called *samke harra* is found in different guises all over the country. It's an ancient recipe for roasted fish served in a spicy tahini sauce (see page 102). Wheat is grown across the mountainous regions and bread-making is an art form. I am particularly fond of the Druze flatbread called *saj*. Bulgur is eaten as a staple carbohydrate. A variety of grades – coarse, fine and extra fine – are used for different dishes: coarse to soak up all the flavours of a pilaf, fine to soften in a classic tabouleh and extra fine mixed with raw minced lamb or goat to make *kibbeh nayyeh*.

Kibbeh is a national obsession. It comes in different shapes and sizes, always using the same base of ground meat and bulgur, from the ultra pared-back raw *kibbeh nayyeh* to a tray-baked version or deep-fried kofta. I asked so many people about the origin of this dish and no one had an exact answer for me. The gist is that *kibbeh* is made with hearty mountain ingredients that are plentiful, and each region has a different style. It's widely believed that the best *kibbeh* comes from Zgharta, a town in the northeast, where I was lucky enough to work with a wonderful local woman called Georgina Bayeh. She taught me how to make

different versions of *kibbeh*, each using the same base of very finely ground lamb, almost whipped and bright pink in colour, mixed with extra fine bulgur. One of her sensational recipes for *kibbeh* is on page 82.

'SAHTAIN'

In Lebanon, people say '*sahtain*' before or after a meal. It literally means 'double health'. What it really refers to is the shared bond of enjoying food. I guess it's like saying to someone: 'Love every mouthful of what you're about to eat.' I adore this concept. All too often we forget that food is a pleasure and should always be savoured. *Saffron in the Souks* is not the definitive guide to Lebanese cuisine in the traditional sense. It's a snapshot of what's going on in the country today. That's why there's a wonderful Iraqi-inspired *kibbeh* that my Lebanese friend Fadia taught me how to make using rice instead of bulgur and a wickedly good Syrian kebab, alongside very traditional home-cooked Lebanese dishes, like *yakhni* (page 122) and *moghrabieh*, a pasta dish of sorts made with tiny semolina dough balls (page 150). I'm all about discovering new recipes and I try as much as possible not to run with dishes that are already widely available, which is why there is no recipe for classic tabouleh or hummus in this book. Instead, I have found a version of tabouleh (page 18) made in the mountains during spring with no tomatoes or parsley. It's incredible. As for hummus, which I adore, I have a similar dish called *malezeye* (page 16) that has more texture and a fresher flavour. It's delicious and I can't wait for you to give it a go. I have, though, included the flatbread salad fattoush (page 21) as it's such an essential side.

I hope you enjoy using this book as much as I did writing it. Cook up a storm, flood the table with my recipes, love every mouthful and, as the Lebanese say, *sahtain*.

MEZE

BEETROOT, RADISH & TARRAGON SALAD

Meze is a popular way of eating in Lebanon, flooding the table with a dazzling display of small dishes to tuck into. These can be a prelude to a main course or served alongside as accompaniments. This is my version of a classic Lebanese beetroot meze, which I've turned into more of a salad with plenty of fresh herbs, beautifully soft beluga lentils and salty feta. This salad goes well with *moutabal*, also pictured here – you can find the recipe on page 20.

SERVES 4 AS PART OF A MEZE

3 beetroots (about 320g),
   cut into wedges
3 tablespoons olive oil,
   plus extra for drizzling
2 spring onions, finely chopped
70g radishes, mandolined
   or thinly sliced
30g walnuts, bashed into
   a rubble
2 handfuls of roughly chopped
   tarragon leaves
2 handfuls of roughly chopped
   mint leaves
400g tin beluga lentils,
   drained and rinsed
½ teaspoon Aleppo pepper flakes
zest and juice of 1 lemon
40g feta
sea salt and freshly ground
   black pepper

1. Preheat the oven to 220°C/200°C fan/gas mark 7. Put the beetroots into a roasting dish and drizzle over 2 tablespoons of the oil. Season with a good pinch of salt and pepper and toss together. Roast for about 1 hour or until tender. Remove from the oven and leave to cool.

2. Tip the beetroots and any juices into a mixing bowl and add the spring onions, radishes, walnuts, most of the herbs, the lentils, Aleppo pepper flakes, lemon zest and juice, remaining olive oil and a pinch of salt and pepper. Mix together really well so that everything gets coated in the dressing.

3. Tip the salad onto a serving plate and crumble over the feta. Scatter with the remaining herbs and drizzle with olive oil before serving.

AKRA SMASHED LEMON CHICKPEAS

[MALEZEYE]

From 6am to 3pm, Akra restaurant in the old souk of Tripoli, Lebanon's second-largest city, celebrates the chickpea, transforming the humble pulse into a series of divine dishes. The restaurant is located in a fabulous old Ottoman building, with seating for up to 350 diners. You can choose from their classic hummus, one with meat, *ful* – a dish of mashed broad beans – and this one. Like the classic hummus recipe, *malezeye* is made with chickpeas, but has more lemon and less tahini. It's not blitzed until completely smooth so there is more texture and it feels somewhat lighter to eat. In the restaurant they serve it covered in nuts for extra crunch, with chewy flatbreads and a plate of herbs and pickles on the side.

SERVES 6 AS PART OF A MEZE

300g (dry weight) chickpeas,
    soaked overnight
½ teaspoon bicarbonate of soda
2 garlic cloves, peeled
120g tahini
juice of 1½ lemons
60g butter
1 teaspoon Aleppo pepper flakes
50g toasted almonds
50g toasted cashew nuts
sea salt

1. Drain the chickpeas in a colander and give them a quick rinse. Tip them into a saucepan and cover with a few inches of cold water. Add the bicarbonate of soda and bring to the boil over a high heat. The bicarbonate of soda causes a mad rush of bubbles, so keep an eye on the pan and skim them off. Once boiling, reduce the heat to low and cook for 1½–2 hours or until the chickpeas are really soft, adding more boiling water if needed. Drain the chickpeas in a colander placed over a mixing bowl to reserve the cooking liquid.

2. Put 150g of the chickpeas into a large mixing bowl and tip the rest into a food-processor. Add the garlic, tahini, 200ml of the cooking liquid, the lemon juice and a really good pinch of salt. Blend into a lumpy-looking dip. If it seems too thick, add a little more of the cooking liquid and pulse together. Transfer to the bowl with the whole chickpeas and mix well.

3. Melt the butter in a small pan over a medium heat. Add the Aleppo pepper flakes and a pinch of salt. Mix well and remove from the heat. Leave for 30 seconds to infuse.

4. Tip the malezeye into a serving bowl and swirl it around with a spoon to spread out. Drizzle with the melted butter and scatter over the nuts. Serve immediately.

CHOUF MOUNTAIN SPRING TABOULEH

This version of tabouleh might seem a tad outrageous. I mean, where is all the tomato and parsley? The tabouleh that we know is a summer recipe, and high in the lush green Chouf Mountains southeast of Beirut, the villagers use what's in season, adapting the dishes they love with the ingredients that taste the best. The version here is prepared in spring when the tomatoes are not quite at peak sweetness. Instead, brown lentils and freshly chopped mint are used, and a little pomegranate molasses added in for a sugary hit. The salad is often served with vine leaves or crisp lettuce leaves for scooping up mouthfuls without bothering with a boring old fork. It's a lovely way to present the tabouleh as part of a meze spread.

SERVES 4 AS PART OF A MEZE

65g bulgur
400g tin brown lentils,
  rinsed and drained
2 large handfuls of finely
  chopped mint leaves
4 spring onions, finely chopped
juice of ½ lemon,
  or more to taste
2 tablespoons pomegranate
  molasses
1 tablespoon olive oil
sea salt

1. Put the bulgur into a pan and cover with just-boiled water. Bring to the boil over a high heat, reduce to a simmer and cook for 5–6 minutes until just tender. Drain, refresh under cold running water and drain again thoroughly.

2. Tip the bulgur, lentils, mint and spring onions into a bowl and add the lemon juice, pomegranate molasses, olive oil and a good pinch of salt. Mix everything together really well and check the balance of flavours. Add more salt or lemon to get it just right.

3. Transfer the tabouleh to a serving bowl and serve immediately.

SMOKED AUBERGINE & TAHINI DIP

[MOUTABAL]

Nestled in the mountainous region of Batroun in north Lebanon, the village of Douma overlooks a lush green valley that stretches down to the azure-blue Mediterranean. It has a laid-back, Tuscan vibe and the cooler climate means Douma is the place to come and chill during the hot summer months. At my friend Kamal Mouzawak's fabulous hotel, Beit Douma, one of the beautiful stone houses scattered around the old Greek Orthodox church, long lazy lunches roll into decadent dinners, served on the terrace with chilled rosé. *Moutabal*, which is more familiar to us under the name baba ganoush, is one of those common dishes that every mum will make in her own style, some adding yogurt and others not. The *moutabal* prepared by Kamal's chef Jemal, a lovely local lady who has been cooking all her life, is quite simply the best. Here it is for you to enjoy. *Pictured on page 14.*

SERVES 4 AS PART OF A MEZE

2 aubergines
70g tahini
juice of 1 lemon
2 tablespoons olive oil
a small handful of finely
    chopped mint leaves
a pinch of sumac
sea salt

1. Place the aubergines straight onto a gas flame and leave to char for about 10–12 minutes, turning them every couple of minutes so that they cook evenly. You want them to look burnt and a little battered on the outside and to be lovely and tender inside. Leave them to cool and then peel off and discard the burnt skin. Finely chop the flesh and add it to a mixing bowl.

2. Using a fork, give the aubergines a good mix to mash into a paste. Add the tahini, lemon juice and salt and mix well. Tip the moutabal onto a serving dish and drizzle over the olive oil. Scatter over the mint and sumac. Serve immediately.

CLASSIC FATTOUSH

This vibrant salad is found all over Lebanon. It's a crunchy mix of freshly chopped vegetables, herbs and fried flatbread – the point being, it's a great way to use up any slightly stale bread. Left to mingle in the dressing, the crisp bread soaks up all the wonderful tart flavours. I have stuck to a very classic medley of veggies, but in Lebanon, the ingredients used will follow the seasons, so feel free to swap things in and out as you like. *Pictured on page 23.*

SERVES 4 AS PART OF A MEZE

vegetable oil, for deep frying
50g flatbread, ripped into
   2.5cm pieces
1–2 Arabic cucumbers or
   ½ regular cucumber,
   deseeded and roughly sliced
200g tomatoes, deseeded
   and roughly chopped
2 spring onions, thinly sliced
1 red pepper, deseeded
   and roughly chopped
100g radishes, thinly sliced
a bunch of roughly chopped
   mint leaves
a bunch of roughly chopped
   parsley leaves
juice of 1 lemon
2 tablespoons olive oil
1 teaspoon sumac
sea salt

1. Heat 5–7cm of oil in a saucepan over a medium heat and deep-fry the bread in two batches for about 1 minute each until golden and crisp. Remove with a slotted spoon and drain on kitchen paper to get rid of any excess oil.

2. Mix together all the remaining ingredients for the salad in a large serving bowl. Make sure that everything gets completely coated in the lovely tart dressing. Scatter over the crispy fried bread and serve immediately.

DIMA'S BULGUR SALAD

Kishk is a Lebanese delicacy made from fermented yogurt, which is dried in the summer sun and then crushed into a fine powder to keep the dairy flavour readily available during the winter months. Its unmistakable and unique taste adds a strong umami flavour to different dishes, from soups to man'ouche flatbreads and even salads. My wonderful friend Dima, a vivacious Syrian chef working in Lebanon, prepared a simple salad that should have used kishk in the base. As she said with a twinkle in her eyes, 'Who's got the time to dry yogurt?' And like that, she made this incredible meze, with nutty bulgur softened in creamy yogurt and strewn with different toppings. I loved her carefree attitude towards cooking. It was fabulous.

SERVES 4 AS PART OF A MEZE

180g bulgur
280g labna (see below),
    plus extra if needed
juice of ½ lemon
35g walnuts, bashed into a rubble
2 spring onions, finely chopped
a handful of finely chopped
    mint leaves
olive oil, for drizzling
sea salt

1. Cook the bulgur for 6–7 minutes in a pan of boiling water until just tender. Drain and refresh under cold running water, then drain again thoroughly. Tip into a mixing bowl and add the labna and lemon juice. Season with salt and mix well. Cover and refrigerate for about 2 hours.

2. Remove the bulgur from the fridge about 20 minutes before serving to allow it to come to room temperature. Mix well and check the seasoning. If the mix is too dry, stir in a few extra tablespoons of labna to loosen. Add most of the walnuts, spring onions and mint and mix well.

3. Transfer to a serving dish and scatter over the remaining walnuts, spring onions and mint leaves. Drizzle over a little olive oil and serve immediately.

HOMEMADE LABNA

Labna is strained yogurt. It's as easy to make as it is to buy. Simply strain some good-quality yogurt (and by that I mean nothing low fat – sorry guys, but if you're going to do it, do it right!) overnight through muslin or a clean cloth suspended over a bowl. The water will drain off the yogurt and you will be left with lusciously thick, creamy labna with an intense flavour.

MAKES 320G

350g full-fat Greek yogurt

1. Line a strainer with a few layers of muslin and place the full-fat yogurt in the centre. Gather the sides of the muslin and twist them around the yogurt, securing into a ball. Put it back in the strainer and place over a bowl. Leave it in the fridge for 12–24 hours so that the liquid drains into the bowl and the yogurt thickens into labna. This will keep for about 1 week in the fridge.

CORIANDER, GARLIC & CHILLI POTATO WEDGES

This killer combination of crispy fried potatoes in a garlicky coriander-and-chilli-spiked dressing is a classic Lebanese meze dish, perfect with the chicken wings on page 27.

SERVES 4 AS PART OF A MEZE

450g baking potatoes,
   skin on, cut into wedges
4 tablespoons olive oil
¼ teaspoon allspice
3 garlic cloves, finely chopped
a handful of finely chopped
   coriander leaves and stalks
1 red chilli, finely chopped
sea salt

1. Preheat the oven to 220°C/200°C fan/gas mark 7. Put the potatoes into a bowl and add 2 tablespoons of the olive oil, the allspice and a good pinch of salt. Toss together and tip onto a roasting tray. Roast for 35–40 minutes until gloriously golden and tender.

2. Heat the remaining oil in a large frying pan over a medium heat. Add the garlic, coriander and chilli and stir-fry for 1 minute until beautifully fragrant. Add the potatoes and toss in the hot oil to absorb all those fragrant flavours. Tip onto a serving plate and serve immediately.

ARMENIAN CUCUMBER SALAD

Armenian food is prevalent in Beirut and you can find so many cracking restaurants in the fashionable neighbourhood of Mar Mikhaël and the lively district of Bourj Hammoud, which is known as 'Little Armenia'. Dishes range from intricate dumplings called *manti* to this simple cucumber salad. Flecked with dried mint, which gives a more floral note than fresh, and doused in lemon juice, this is a fantastic dish to serve as part of a meze. Arabic cucumbers are much smaller than the traditional ones and have a stronger flavour, but they are by no means essential for this salad. If you can't find them, you can use a regular cucumber – just halve lengthways, scrape out the seeds and cut into half moons.

SERVES 4 AS PART OF A MEZE

juice of ½ lemon
2 tablespoons olive oil
5 teaspoons dried mint
2–3 Arabic cucumbers, sliced,
   or 1 regular cucumber,
   deseeded and sliced
sea salt

1. In a large mixing bowl, whisk together the lemon, olive oil, dried mint and a good pinch of salt to make a dressing. Add the cucumber and toss well. Cover and put in the fridge for 20–30 minutes for the flavours to develop. Give the salad a quick mix before serving.

GARLIC CHICKEN WINGS WITH CORIANDER & PISTACHIO PESTO

[JAWANEH]

These finger-licking chicken wings or *jawaneh* are a staple Lebanese meze dish. Marinating them overnight in a simple mix of yogurt, lemon and garlic tenderises the meat beautifully. Although delicious with just a squeeze of lemon, I like to give the wings a little more oomph and serve mine with a fragrant coriander and pistachio pesto. This vibrant green concoction looks impressive, but it's simple to make and the flavour works perfectly with tasty charred chicken.

SERVES 4 AS PART OF A MEZE

For the wings
4 garlic cloves, peeled
½ teaspoon allspice
juice of ½ lemon
2 tablespoons Greek yogurt
500g chicken wings
1 tablespoon olive oil
sea salt

For the pesto
10g pistachio kernels
2 handfuls of roughly chopped
   coriander leaves
2 tablespoons white wine vinegar
1 tablespoon olive oil
sea salt

1. Bash the garlic with a little salt into a paste and tip into a large mixing bowl. Add the allspice, lemon and yogurt and mix well. Tip in the chicken wings and toss together so that the marinade coats the chicken completely. Cover and refrigerate overnight.

2. Preheat the oven to 220°C/200°C fan/gas mark 7 and take the wings out of the fridge to come to room temperature. Pour the olive oil over the wings and mix well. Transfer to a baking tray and roast for 35–40 minutes until golden and gnarly.

3. Meanwhile, bash the pistachios and coriander into a rough paste. Pour in the vinegar and olive oil and season with a pinch of salt. Mix this together really well and serve immediately alongside the wings.

CHILLI & GARLIC PICKLED AUBERGINES
[MAKDOUS]

The Lebanese palate loves a tart tang and these aubergines tickle the taste buds beautifully. During the long hot summer months, baby aubergines are boiled until just tender, stuffed with garlic, walnuts and chilli – a perfect combination of flavour and texture – and then stored in oil for at least a few weeks. Kitchen alchemy occurs and the aubergines start to ferment in the oil, taking on a slightly sour flavour that is utterly addictive and unlike anything I've tasted before. You can serve them whole as part of a meze, chop them into salads or, if you're feeling particularly wicked, turn them into the ultimate mid-morning snack by serving them on flatbread spread with Rose Petal Labna, also pictured here – you can find the recipe on page 32.

SERVES 8 AS PART OF A MEZE

8–12 baby aubergines
  (about 500g)
plenty of sea salt, for pickling
4 garlic cloves, peeled
1 red chilli, roughly chopped
60g walnuts
150ml olive oil

1. Cut a small (1–2cm) slit lengthways into the side of each aubergine and then put them into a pan of boiling water. They will float, so you need to put a bowl or plate over the top to keep them submerged in the water. Cook for 20–25 minutes until tender. Drain through a colander and leave for 5 minutes to cool down.

2. Once cool enough to touch, rub a little salt into the slits you made in the aubergines and place them back in the colander in a layer, slit side down. Put a bowl on top to gently weigh them down. Leave for 2 hours so that the excess moisture drains out of the aubergines.

3. Meanwhile, put the garlic and chilli into a mini food-processor and blend until fine. Add the walnuts and whizz up until fairly fine. Stuff a small amount of the mixture into the slit of each aubergine and place in a 630g sterilised jar – you want them all to fit snugly. Pour over enough oil to just cover everything; you might need a little more or less than the amount given, depending on the size of your aubergines. Seal and leave in a cool, dry place for at least two weeks. Once ready, they'll keep for a few weeks.

ROSE PETAL LABNA

The luscious flavour of labna works so well in both sweet and savoury dishes. It's fabulous dolloped on French toast or porridge, with running honey oozing over the top, or stirred into a lamb stew to enrich the sauce. But it's also incredible on its own as a meze dish with loads of garnishes scattered over the top for texture and a generous glug of olive oil. This rose petal version is fragrant and delicious, while the toasted nuts add texture. It's great with the pickled aubergines on page 30. *Pictured on page 31.*

SERVES 4 AS PART OF A MEZE

320g labna (see page 24)
1 tablespoon olive oil
10g toasted flaked almonds
15g toasted cashew nuts
10g toasted pine nuts
20g sultanas
½ teaspoon sumac
zest of ½ lemon
1 teaspoon dried rose petals

1. Put the labna on a plate, swirl with a spoon and drizzle over the olive oil. Scatter the nuts, sultanas, sumac, lemon zest and rose petals over the top and serve your luscious labna immediately.

SPINACH WITH GARLIC & LEMON

This dish is a spin on a very classic meze made with *hindbeh* or chicory. In Lebanon when the rains come at the start of winter the *hindbeh* shoot up. It's very different from the bitter Belgium chicory bulb: a long, thin, leafy green, more like dandelion leaves, that has a lovely sweet taste once cooked down. Spinach is a reasonable substitute, with that slight tinny taste that works so well with garlic and lemon. Do serve this at room temperature because the flavour develops into something so much more interesting than when hot.

SERVES 4 AS PART OF A MEZE

2 tablespoons olive oil
1 onion, finely chopped
3 garlic cloves, sliced
200g baby spinach
juice of ½ lemon
sea salt and freshly ground
    black pepper

1. Heat the oil in a frying pan over a medium heat and add the onion. Cook, stirring occasionally, for 5–6 minutes until soft. Add the garlic and stir-fry for 30 seconds until fragrant.

2. Add all the spinach to the pan and pour over 2 tablespoons of water. Season with salt and pepper and add half the lemon juice. Stir-fry for 3–4 minutes until wilted. Transfer the spinach to a serving dish and leave to cool completely. Add the remaining lemon juice and mix well. Check the salt and serve immediately.

STICKY POMEGRANATE SUJUK

Sujuk is a rather bulbous beef sausage that you can buy in Middle Eastern stores. It has a lovely smoky flavour and it crisps up beautifully when cooked. To make this recipe more accessible I have developed a home-cooked *sujuk* that tastes just as divine. The rich meat works so well with the sweet-sour tang of pomegranate molasses, which binds everything together into a rather elegant-looking meze.

SERVES 4 AS PART OF A MEZE

260g minced beef with
   20 per cent fat
3 garlic cloves, crushed
1 teaspoon Aleppo pepper flakes
½ teaspoon allspice
½ teaspoon paprika
2 tablespoons olive oil
4 tablespoons pomegranate
   molasses
2 tablespoons slivered
   pistachio nuts
15g pomegranate seeds
a few finely chopped mint
   leaves, to serve
sea salt

1. Mix together the beef, garlic, Aleppo pepper flakes, allspice and paprika in a bowl with a good pinch of salt. Divide into eight and roll each one into a thin sausage shape.

2. Heat the oil in a large non-stick frying pan over a medium heat and fry the sujuk for 5–6 minutes, turning every couple of minutes until golden and just cooked through. Turn the heat off and pour over the pomegranate molasses. Toss everything in the pan so that the sujuk are coated in the molasses and then transfer to a serving dish. Scatter over the pistachios, pomegranate seeds and mint leaves. Serve immediately.

STUFFED VINE LEAVES

[WARAK ARISH]

Found all over Lebanon, *warak arish* are stuffed vine leaves. The leaves from the grape vine are picked, the stems removed and the leaves boiled to make them more malleable to work with. I use brined leaves that I buy in a Middle Eastern store. You have to give them a really good wash in cold water so that they are not too salty. The vine leaves are rolled up like little cigars around a filling – there are so many different types of filling, but often you'll find it's lamb and rice – and cooked low and slow in stock. The *warak arish* have such a lovely mellow tang and are brilliant on a table filled with other meze dishes. They are quite time consuming to prepare, so make like they do in Lebanon and get some tea, grab a mate to help and have a good gossip whilst you whip up a batch.

SERVES 10 AS PART OF A MEZE

60g Basmati rice
180g minced lamb with
    10–15 per cent fat
¼ teaspoon allspice
45 brined vine leaves
1 tomato, sliced
2–3 garlic cloves, peeled
juice of ½ lemon
700ml lamb stock (made
    with ½ a stock cube)
sea salt

1. Wash the rice in cold water to rinse out any excess starch. Drain well, then mix the rice with the lamb, allspice and a good pinch of salt in a mixing bowl.

2. Rinse the vine leaves thoroughly to remove all salty brine and leave to drain in a colander. Place a vine leaf on a chopping board with the stalk end facing you. Put a large teaspoon of the rice mixture on the leaf just above where the stalk would be. Arrange into a line horizontally across the leaf. Fold the sides over the mixture and roll the leaf up from the bottom, keeping it as tight as possible, into a cigar shape. Repeat with the rest. You should be able to make 35–40 warak arish.

3. Cover the base of a non-stick saucepan with 4–5 vine leaves. Arrange the tomato in a layer and put the warak arish on top. Depending on the size of your pan, you can layer them up. Add the garlic and pour over the lemon juice and stock. The stock should cover everything.

4. Bring to the boil over a high heat. Reduce the heat to low and cover the warak arish with an inverted plate to keep them submerged in the stock. Simmer gently for 1½ hours to cook the rice and meat. Take the warak arish out of the liquid and leave to cool. Serve at room temperature.

SIZZLING SUMMER TUNA

The sensational seafood I ate along the glistening coastline of Lebanon inspired my tuna meze. Fish is often cooked straight over a barbecue and served simply with lemon, allowing its freshness to speak for itself. Labna might not seem an obvious pairing for tuna, but the creaminess works well with the meaty flavour of the fish. When you cook your tuna, flash-fry it so it's still pink in the middle. If you're firing up the barbecue, you can also sear a whole tuna steak and then dice it up afterwards.

SERVES 4 AS PART OF A MEZE

4 tablespoons olive oil
4 garlic cloves, thinly sliced
a small handful of finely
    chopped coriander leaves
240g yellowfin tuna,
    cut into 1cm chunks
juice of ½ lemon
200g labna (see page 24)
1 teaspoon sumac
½ teaspoon Aleppo pepper flakes
sea salt

1. Heat the oil in a frying pan over a high heat and add the garlic and coriander. Stir-fry for 20 seconds until fragrant. Add the tuna and season with a good pinch of salt. Mix well and stir-fry for about 1 minute until half cooked. Remove the pan from the heat, squeeze in the lemon juice and mix well.

2. Swirl the labna onto a serving dish and top with the tuna. Drizzle over all the juices from the pan. Scatter over the sumac and Aleppo pepper flakes. Serve immediately.

CRISPY ZA'ATAR CALAMARI

Fabulous seafood restaurants are dotted along the entire length of Lebanon's coastline and they all serve great platters of calamari, crispy and golden, with huge wedges of lemon to squeeze over the top before devouring them. This is such a simple recipe with the piping hot fried squid tossed in a little za'atar and salt to give even more flavour to the seafood.

SERVES 4 AS PART OF A MEZE

vegetable oil, for deep-frying
400g squid tubes
3 tablespoons cornflour
3 tablespoons plain flour
2 tablespoons za'atar
lemon wedges, to serve
sea salt

1. Heat 7–10cm of oil in a saucepan over a high heat. Pat the squid tubes dry with kitchen paper and cut into 1cm lengths.

2. Mix the cornflour and plain flour in a bowl. Working in three or four batches, toss the squid in the flour and then put a batch straight into the hot oil. (Don't leave any squid standing in flour otherwise it becomes soggy.) Leave to bubble furiously for 2–3 minutes. Once the bubbles die down and the squid looks golden and crispy, remove with a slotted spoon and drain on kitchen paper. Repeat with the remaining squid.

3. Put the za'atar into a bowl and add a good pinch of salt. Add the cooked squid and toss together. Serve immediately with the lemon wedges.

VEGETABLES

GRIDDLED AUBERGINE FATTEH

This is my version of the heavenly Lebanese layered dish aubergine *fatteh*. Traditionally, aubergines are roasted or fried in chunks and then completely covered in a rich tahini sauce. This luscious layer of sesame goodness is then showered in different toppings to add colour, flavour and texture. As I travelled around the country, I spotted nuances in the way *fatteh* is prepared. In Baalbek in the east, for example, they add tangy pomegranate molasses to the tahini sauce, which gives it a lighter touch, and use fragrant dried mint as a garnish. It is a delicious dish, but I can't help but feel that the sauce overpowers the aubergines. For mine, I have continued down the lighter route, griddling whole slices of aubergine and then layering them up with a drizzle of the rich sauce over the top. I love a garnish and have not held back. *Fatteh* would be served as a part of a large meal, but frankly it's wonderful on its own with flatbread and mint tea.

SERVES 4

vegetable oil, for deep-frying
50g flatbread, ripped into
    2.5cm pieces
2 aubergines, sliced lengthways
    into 5mm slices
4 tablespoons olive oil,
    plus extra for drizzling
juice of 1 lemon
100g Greek yogurt
55g tahini
1 garlic clove, crushed
sea salt

To garnish
25g toasted pine nuts
50g pomegranate seeds
a small handful of
    coriander leaves

1. Heat 7–10cm of oil in a saucepan over a medium heat and deep-fry the bread for about 1 minute until golden and crisp. Remove with a slotted spoon and drain on kitchen paper to remove the excess oil.

2. Heat a griddle pan over a high heat. Brush both sides of the aubergine slices with olive oil and season with salt. Griddle for 2–3 minutes on each side until charred and tender. I find one side always takes longer and one side cooks much quicker. Just keep an eye on them and if they're cooking too quickly, reduce the heat a little. Place on a serving plate and squeeze over half the lemon juice.

3. Meanwhile mix together the yogurt, tahini, 50ml of the water, garlic and the remaining lemon to a smooth dressing. Spoon over the aubergines. Garnish with the pine nuts, pomegranate seeds, fried bread and coriander. Drizzle over a little olive oil and serve immediately.

ORZO & FETA STUFFED PEPPERS

This recipe is a play on my friend Rima Khodr's signature dish, *horr osbaa*. The original recipe is a brilliant brown stew made with lentils, garlic and a generous amount of pomegranate molasses. Traditionally this would be carb'ed up with tiny pasta-like dumplings that mellow in the stew, but to give it a more modern feel she uses orzo. I loved the dish and have used all the flavours and ingredients to make my stuffed peppers. They look beautiful and the vibrant green coriander dressing makes everything pop even more.

SERVES 4

2 large or 4 small red
  peppers, halved
4 tablespoons olive oil
120g orzo
300g tin green lentils, drained
2 spring onions, finely chopped
2 tablespoons pomegranate
  molasses
120g cherry tomatoes, halved
60g feta
½ garlic clove
a handful of roughly chopped
  coriander leaves and stalks
juice of ½ lemon
15g toasted pine nuts
sea salt

1. Preheat the oven to 200°C/180°C fan/gas mark 6. Put the peppers in a roasting dish and rub 2 tablespoons of the oil all over them. Season with salt and roast for 40–45 minutes until golden and tender. Transfer to a serving dish and set aside.

2. Meanwhile, drop the orzo into a pan of boiling water. Stir well to stop it sticking and cook for 6–8 minutes until tender but still with a little bite. Drain and refresh under cold running water. Drain again and tip into a mixing bowl. Add the lentils, spring onions, pomegranate molasses and 1 tablespoon of the olive oil. Season with salt and mix well. Stuff the cooked peppers with the mix and spoon the remaining orzo around them. Arrange the cherry tomatoes and feta over the top.

3. Bash the garlic with a little salt into a paste. Add the coriander and bash again into a paste. Add the lemon juice, remaining olive oil and 1 tablespoon of water. Mix into a dressing and drizzle over the stuffed peppers. Scatter over the pine nuts and serve immediately.

MONASTERY OF THE MOON CABBAGE

I was invited to the summer opening of a stunning little hotel in the Chouf region, just above the stone village of Deir El Qamar, which means 'Monastery of the Moon'. The village is built around a wonderful old square with a little mosque and a few quiet terraces to enjoy a cool drink. I arrived at the hotel's restaurant early to see the chefs at work and obviously ended up helping with service. They were making a feast with great piles of kebabs, rich stews, fluffy rice, meze and a table of mouth-watering desserts. But one of the standout recipes was a simple dish of braised cabbage mixed with fine bulgur and spices: it was utterly delicious. The combination of tomato, lemon and dried mint epitomises East Mediterranean cooking for me. Again I have to thank my friend Dima for this recipe. Babe, it rocks!

SERVES 4 AS A SIDE

3 tablespoons olive oil
1 onion, finely sliced
500g white cabbage, finely sliced
1 teaspoon dried mint
juice of 1½ lemons
1 tablespoon tomato purée
20g extra fine bulgur
a large handful of finely
   chopped mint leaves
sea salt

1. Heat 2 tablespoons of the oil in a large frying pan over a medium heat and add the onion. Cook, stirring occasionally, for 6–8 minutes until soft.

2. Crank the heat up to high and put the cabbage into the pan with the onion. Stir-fry for 2–3 minutes to start the cooking process and then pour 50ml of water into the pan. Continue to stir-fry for 30 seconds. Cover, reduce the heat to low and cook for 7–8 minutes until the cabbage is softened, but still has a little bite.

3. Remove the pan from the heat. Tip in the dried mint and add a third of the lemon juice, the tomato purée, bulgur and a further 50ml of water. Mix this together really well and then cover the pan. Leave it to rest for 30 minutes so that the bulgur can soften and absorb all the flavours.

4. Squeeze the remaining lemon juice into the pan and add the last of the olive oil. Mix well to wake everything up. Check the salt and season to taste. Add the chopped mint and toss together. Transfer to a serving dish and serve at room temperature.

ROASTED CARROTS WITH TAHINI & BLACK SESAME SEEDS

One of the big flavours used in Lebanese cooking is tahini, a rich paste made from roasted and ground sesame seeds. When buying tahini, make sure it has a lovely pale colour and is really glossy and pourable. It should feel silken and smooth on your tongue and taste a little sweet, never bitter. Supermarkets have limited options; often you'll find tahini in a jar with a layer of oil on the top – this is just the natural oil split from the sesame seeds. If this is all you can buy, you need to open the jar and give everything a really good stir to return it to a thin, even-textured paste. If the taste is bitter, mix a little yogurt into your tahini to soften it. The Lebanese use tahini for so much more than hummus, adding it to salads, stews and gorgeous desserts. Here, it turns simple roasted carrots into a sophisticated side dish. Winner.

SERVES 4 AS A SIDE

450g heritage carrots
2 tablespoons olive oil
¾ teaspoon ground cumin
juice of ½ lemon
3 tablespoons tahini
a small handful of finely
  chopped coriander leaves
½ teaspoon black sesame seeds
sea salt

1. Preheat the oven to 220°C/200°C fan/gas mark 7. Tip the carrots into a roasting dish and pour over the olive oil. Season with salt and the cumin. Toss together and roast for 30–35 minutes or until tender.

2. Transfer to a serving dish and squeeze over the lemon. Gently mix together. Drizzle over the tahini and scatter the coriander and sesame seeds on top. Serve immediately.

MIGHTY MEDINA FALAFEL SANDWICH

South along the coast from Beirut is the ancient Phoenician port of Saida, or Sidon. The city is known for its street food and I ended up scouring the sun-soaked medina and sampling incredible cuisine among the heaving hummus stalls and sizzling shawarma bars. But the dish of the day went to the restaurant Falafel Akkawi Saida, which serves the best falafel sandwich in the medina. They nailed it; the combination of crispy fried falafel, creamy condiments, crunchy salad and tangy pickles was out of this world.

MAKES 6–8 PITTAS

For the falafel
1 onion, roughly chopped
4 garlic cloves, peeled
a large handful of coriander
    leaves and stalks
a large handful of parsley leaves
400g chickpeas, soaked
    overnight in cold water
    and drained
4 tablespoons gram flour
2 teaspoons ground cumin
2 teaspoons ground coriander
1 teaspoon Aleppo pepper flakes
½ teaspoon baking powder
¼ teaspoon bicarbonate of soda
vegetable oil, for deep-frying
sea salt

To serve
6–8 round pitta breads, split
2 Baby Gem lettuce, finely sliced
2 handfuls of parsley leaves
200g pickles, thinly sliced
2 teaspoons sumac
tahini, to drizzle
chilli sauce, to taste

1. Blitz the onion and garlic in a food-processer until fine. Add the herbs and continue to blend until they are completely whizzed up. Add the chickpeas, gram flour, cumin, coriander, Aleppo pepper flakes, baking powder and bicarbonate of soda. Season with a really good pinch of salt and blitz again for a few minutes to combine. Scrape the sides down with a spatula and blend until the mixture combines into a paste. Roll into 30–32 small falafel the size of walnuts.

2. Heat the vegetable oil in a deep saucepan over a medium–high heat. You will need about 7–10cm oil, enough to completely cover your falafel. Cook the falafel, a few at a time, for 1–2 minutes until golden. You have to watch the heat, adjusting it so that they don't cook too fast and burn. Remove with a slotted spoon and drain on kitchen paper.

3. Serve in the pitta with lettuce, parsley, pickles, a sprinkle of sumac, a drizzle of tahini and chilli sauce to taste.

FARM TABLE TOMATO SALAD

This simple salad showcases the sweet summer tomatoes that are grown all over Lebanon. Like most Mediterranean countries, Lebanese produce is incredible. The fruits and vegetables soak up the glorious sunshine and have the best flavour. As with any good ingredients, you don't have to do much. To make my rustic salad, simply choose a vibrant selection of tomatoes in all different shapes, colours and sizes, and cut them randomly. The hint of vinegar and sumac gives the sweet fruit a little hum to further enliven the dish.

SERVES 4–6 AS A SIDE

2 garlic cloves
2 tablespoons olive oil
1 tablespoon red wine vinegar
500g different sized and
   coloured tomatoes, sliced
   into rounds (or halves/quarters
   for small tomatoes)
sea salt and freshly ground
   black pepper

To *garnish*
20g toasted pine nuts
½ teaspoon sumac
a small handful of torn
   mint leaves

1. Put the garlic into a pestle and mortar with a little salt and bash into a paste. Add the olive oil and red wine vinegar and mix into a lovely thick dressing.

2. Arrange the tomatoes on a serving plate and season with a little salt and pepper. Drizzle the dressing over the top and garnish the tomatoes with pine nuts, sumac and mint leaves. Serve immediately.

WHOLE ROASTED HALLOUMI & CITRUS SALAD

The first time I discovered whole roasted halloumi in Lebanon I fell in love with it. It's such a great way to cook the cheese. I am not going to knock pan-fried slices because they are equally delicious, but it's just wonderful to discover a new way of cooking a favourite food. The whole block of cheese is pan-fried to give a lovely colour on all sides and then roasted to soften. When the halloumi comes out of the oven it looks super relaxed, as if it has just exhaled happily, and when you poke it you can feel the cheese give in a moreish, melted way. The rest of the ingredients are sensational summer foods: citrus fruits and soft herbs. This is best enjoyed outside on a sunny terrace.

SERVES 2 AS A MAIN OR 4 AS A SIDE

2 tablespoons olive oil
250g block of halloumi
1 grapefruit, peeled
2 oranges, peeled
60g mixed rocket and
    baby spinach
2 handfuls of fresh
    oregano leaves
sea salt

To garnish
10g pistachio kernels, bashed
    into a rubble
1 teaspoon sumac
½ teaspoon Aleppo pepper flakes

1. Preheat the oven to 200°C/180°C fan/gas mark 6. Heat the oil in a small, non-stick, ovenproof frying pan. Add the block of halloumi and cook for 2–3 minutes until golden on one side and then cook the four smaller sides for 30–40 seconds each until golden. Flip the block of halloumi onto its uncooked side and place the pan in the oven and roast for 18–20 minutes until the halloumi is really soft and gooey. The top will sink a little and when you poke the cheese in the middle, it should feel really soft.

2. Meanwhile, segment the grapefruit and oranges over a bowl to catch all the juices. Add a little salt to the juices and whisk them together. Put the segmented pieces of fruit into the bowl with the juices and add the salad leaves and half the oregano. Toss together and arrange on a serving plate. Place the gloriously golden block of cheese in the middle and garnish with the pistachios, sumac, Aleppo pepper flakes and remaining oregano. Serve immediately.

PURSLANE, POMEGRANATE & ROASTED COURGETTES

Purslane, or *bakleh*, is a wonderful wild weed that loves sunlight and grows particularly well in Lebanon. It has light red stems and pert, green leaves that have a mellow citrus tang. You can eat the leaves raw in a salad or mixed with labna, or cook them down with onions and sumac to stuff into pastries. Loaded with vitamins and omega-3, purslane is really nutritious. In this recipe the leaves add a fresh, crunchy layer to this typically Lebanese salad made with loads of vegetables in a tangy dressing, enriched with a drizzle of tahini. If you can't find purslane, try using lamb's lettuce instead. It has a similar look and feel, but is perhaps not quite so tart.

SERVES 4

900g courgettes, cut into
   2.5–3cm rounds
3 tablespoons olive oil
250g cherry tomatoes,
   roughly chopped
4 spring onions, roughly sliced
juice of 1 lemon
90g purslane
1 tablespoon pomegranate
   molasses
2 tablespoons tahini
10g toasted pine nuts
sea salt and freshly ground
   black pepper

1. Preheat the oven to 200°C/180°C fan/gas mark 6. Put the courgettes into a roasting tray, pour over 2 tablespoons of the olive oil and season well with salt and pepper. Toss together and roast for 40–45 minutes until golden and tender. Leave to cool, then tip into a serving dish.

2. Put the tomatoes and spring onions into a mixing bowl. Add the lemon juice, remaining olive oil and a good pinch of salt and pepper. Toss together and scatter over the courgettes.

3. Put the purslane into the same bowl you used to dress the tomatoes and toss in the remaining juices. Transfer to the serving dish and arrange over the top of the tomatoes. Spoon over any remaining juices from the bowl.

4. Drizzle the pomegranate molasses and tahini over the top of the purslane, then scatter over the pine nuts. Serve immediately.

JACQUELINE'S SMOKY AUBERGINES

After a particularly long day hiking in the incredibly beautiful Qadisha Valley, I stayed in a local guesthouse called Dar Qadisha run by Jacqueline Touma. The building was old, with huge stone arches, vaulted ceilings and ornate balconies. Pastel-coloured roses grew all around Jacqueline's garden, hugging the sides of the house. Without me knowing, she had prepared dinner, which was the perfect ending to a long day exploring the valley: sizzling *shish taouk* (kebabs), cumin-heavy hummus, freshly made bread and a tangy aubergine salad. Aubergines are engrained in the Lebanese diet and are so versatile that they feature in a number of different dishes including *moutabal* (see page 20) and aubergine *fatteh* (see page 46). Jacqueline served hers lightly charred for a smoky flavour and chopped to a rough paste, then mixed with fresh ingredients.

SERVES 4 AS A SIDE

2 aubergines
300g different coloured cherry
    tomatoes, roughly chopped
4 spring onions, finely sliced
2 handfuls of roughly chopped
    mint leaves
2 tablespoons olive oil
juice of 1 lemon
sea salt

1. Put the aubergines straight onto a gas flame and leave to char for about 8–10 minutes. Turn them every couple of minutes so that they cook evenly. You want them to look burnt and a little battered on the outside and to be tender but still with a little texture on the inside. Leave them to cool and then peel off and discard the burnt skin.

2. Roughly chop the flesh and transfer to a mixing bowl. Add the tomatoes, spring onions and mint. Season with a good pinch of salt and pour in the olive oil and lemon juice. Mix everything thoroughly, then tip onto a serving plate.

PEA & MINT STUFFED ARTICHOKES

This is such a simple dish of little artichoke hearts stuffed with lemony, minted peas – knockout summer food. When artichokes are not in season or I want to make this with minimum effort, I buy artichoke hearts in oil and just drain them. But when artichokes are in season and I have the time, I'll cook them fresh. A lovely tip I picked up in Lebanon is to add a whole bunch of fresh mint to the pan while the artichokes boil, which perfumes them as they cook in the pot.

SERVES 4 AS A SIDE

150g frozen peas
juice of 1 lemon
2 tablespoons olive oil
a small handful of finely
    chopped mint leaves
8 artichoke hearts in oil,
    drained (160g approx.)
sea salt

1. Cook the peas for 1 minute in a pan of boiling water. Drain, refresh under cold running water, then drain again. Tip into a mixing bowl and add the lemon juice, olive oil, mint and a good pinch of salt. Toss together to coat the peas completely in the tangy dressing.

2. Arrange the artichoke hearts on a plate and fill each one with the peas. Spoon over any dressing left in the bowl and serve immediately.

CREAMY SPINACH & PUMPKIN KIBBEH

Traditional *kibbeh* is a blend of bulgur and ground lamb. Like everything, cooking evolves and catches up with modern-day palates, and now you can find exquisite vegetarian *kibbeh* served all over the country. In Beirut I ate pumpkin *kibbeh* that had been tray baked in layers with spinach. I created my own version using roasted pumpkin and bulgur as the base for the little kofta shapes and stuffing them with creamy spinach filling. If you can't find pumpkin, you can use squash instead.

SERVES 4

500g peeled pumpkin,
    cut into 2.5–5cm pieces
5 tablespoons olive oil,
    plus extra for drizzling
¼ teaspoon ground cinnamon
¼ teaspoon allspice
100g extra fine bulgur
300g spinach leaves
1 onion, finely chopped
2 garlic cloves, finely chopped
a handful of finely chopped
    parsley leaves, plus a few
    leaves for garnish
1¼ teaspoons sumac
200g labna (see page 24)
20g toasted pine nuts
vegetable oil, for deep frying
juice of ½ lemon
¼ teaspoon Aleppo pepper flakes
sea salt and freshly ground
    black pepper

1. Preheat the oven to 220°C/200°C fan/gas mark 7. Put the pumpkin into a bowl. Add 1 tablespoon of the olive oil and season generously. Toss together and tip onto a roasting tray. Roast for 25–30 minutes. Leave to cool, then transfer to a mixing bowl. Add the cinnamon and allspice and mash together until smooth. Check the seasoning and adjust if needed.

2. Soak the bulgur in 2 tablespoons of water for 5 minutes and then add to the pumpkin. Mix well. Cover and refrigerate for 1 hour to firm up.

3. Meanwhile, heat a large frying pan over a high heat. Add half the spinach, a good pinch of salt and 1 tablespoon of water. Stir-fry for 1½–2 minutes until completely wilted. Transfer to a sieve and repeat with the remaining spinach. Using the back of a spoon, push the spinach to get all the excess water out. Tip onto a chopping board and finely chop.

4. Heat 2 tablespoons of the olive oil in a pan over a medium heat and add the onion. Cook, stirring occasionally, for 5–6 minutes until soft. Add the garlic and stir-fry for 30 seconds until fragrant. Add this to the spinach, along with the chopped parsley, 1 teaspoon of the sumac, 80g of the labna and 10g of the pine nuts. Mix well and season.

5. Divide the pumpkin into 12 portions and roll into balls. Using your thumb, make a well in one of the balls and add a little of the spinach mixture. Close up the hole and roll back into a ball. Place on a plate lined with cling film. Repeat with the rest. You should use up about half the spinach mixture. Cover and refrigerate for 15 minutes to firm up.

6. Heat 7–10cm oil in a deep saucepan over a medium-high heat. You will need enough oil to completely cover the kibbeh. Fry the kibbeh, in batches, for 1–1½ minutes until golden. Drain on kitchen paper.

7. Mix the remaining spinach, labna, and olive oil with the lemon juice and a good pinch of salt. Swirl onto a serving dish and top with the cooked kibbeh. Sprinkle with Aleppo pepper flakes, parsley and the remaining sumac and pinenuts, then drizzle with olive oil and serve.

GARLICKY DOUMA DUMPLINGS

I didn't expect to be eating dumplings in Lebanon, but there I was in the pretty village of Douma feasting on *maakroun btoum*, which means pasta with garlic. Slightly more gnocchi like than pasta, these pillowy soft dumplings had been cleverly rolled against the fine side of a cheese grater to curl them up, cooked and then dunked in a garlic, lemon and oil emulsion. It was exquisite – rustic food that felt so refined, as I often feel about really good home-cooked meals. In fact, so enamoured was I by my first mouthful that the teenager in me wanted an Instagram pic with the wild-flower garden in the background. It's all about the background. So I rushed, dish in hand, to go outside, sadly missing the fact that the glass sliding doors had been closed. Bam! *Maakroun btoum* all over me, and my local audience in hysterics.

SERVES 4

For the dough
300g plain flour, plus
   extra for dusting
1 teaspoon (3.5g)
   fast-action yeast
1 teaspoon salt
2 tablespoons olive oil
250ml warm water

For the sauce
4 garlic cloves, crushed
6 tablespoons olive oil
zest of 1 lemon and juice
   of 1½ lemons
1½ teaspoons sugar
2 handfuls of finely chopped
   mint leaves
sea salt

1. Put the flour, yeast and salt into a bowl and mix together. Add the olive oil and water and bring together into a dough. Knead on a floured surface until smooth. Roll into a sausage and divide into 16 portions. Cover with clingfilm while you work to prevent the dough drying out. Roll out one portion so that it's about 10cm long and then cut it into eight small pieces. Repeat with the rest and dust them all with flour. Dust the fine side of a cheese grater with flour and then carefully roll each piece of dough against the grater using your forefingers. Push down as you go so that the dough presses against the holes of the grater and curls up as you pull it down. You get a lovely textured curve, a little like calamari, which is great for holding loads of the fragrant sauce.

2. Bring a large pan of water to the boil over a high heat and cook the dumplings, in two batches, for about 4–5 minutes. Once cooked, they will have a firmish texture and the flavour of the flour should be cooked out. Drain and leave in the colander, reserving some of the starchy dumpling water for the sauce.

3. Meanwhile, make the sauce. Using a small food-processor, blend the garlic, olive oil, lemon juice, sugar and a pinch of salt until emulsified into a pale, glossy sauce. Tip into a mixing bowl and add the dumplings and half the mint. Pour in 3–4 tablespoons of the reserved dumpling water and a good pinch of salt. Mix well so that you have a lovely sauce that clings to the dumplings. Leave to rest for 2–3 minutes to help thicken the sauce. Transfer to serving bowls and garnish with the remaining mint and lemon zest. Serve immediately.

TRIPOLIAN OKRA STEW

[BAMIEH BIL ZEIT]

This wonderfully tangy okra stew is typical of the bold style of Lebanese cooking. My version is adapted from a Tripolian recipe that's heavy on tart pomegranate molasses and uses whole shallots for texture. You can use either normal okra or baby okra if you can find them. Both have the curse of going sticky unless they are prepped properly. Roasting the okra in the oven first stops the stew from becoming gooey and is a healthier method than the traditional, but rather delicious, option of deep-frying.

SERVES 4

300g okra, halved lengthways
3 tablespoons olive oil
4 echalion (banana) shallots, peeled and halved
6 garlic cloves, peeled
3 tomatoes, finely chopped
1 tablespoon tomato purée
3 tablespoons pomegranate molasses
sea salt

1. Preheat the oven to 220°C/200°C fan/gas mark 7. Tip the okra into a baking tray and pour over 1 tablespoon of the oil. Season with salt and mix well. Roast for 12–15 minutes, shaking the pan halfway through, until the okra have wilted.

2. Meanwhile, heat the remaining oil in a saucepan over a high heat. Add the shallots and garlic and mix well. Reduce the heat to medium and cook, stirring occasionally, for 8–10 minutes until golden.

3. Add the tomatoes and tomato purée to the pan. Pour in 100ml of just-boiled water and add a good pinch of salt. Mix well and cook, stirring occasionally, for 7–8 minutes or until the tomatoes have broken down into a sauce.

4. Transfer the okra to the pan with the sauce. Add the pomegranate molasses and mix well. Check the seasoning and add salt to taste. Cover, reduce the heat to low and cook for 5 minutes to allow the fabulous flavours to mingle. Serve immediately.

SYRIAN SPAGHETTI WITH POMEGRANATE & LENTILS

[HURRAK OSBAO]

The exquisite cuisine of Syria, Lebanon's sadly war-torn neighbour, is found all over the country, wonderfully helping to preserve its ancient food culture. This rather sensational pasta and lentil dish is called *Hurrak Osbao*, which means 'burnt fingers', in reference to it being so damn tasty you can't help but go straight in with your hands. Although I have used more pasta than is traditional (hands up the pasta fiend!), the flavours are spot on, combining fragrant coriander, dried mint, cumin and tangy pomegranate molasses. Despite being very distinct tasting ingredients, they marry together beautifully in this dish.

SERVES 4

200g fettuccine
4 tablespoons olive oil,
    plus extra for drizzling
2 onions, finely sliced
4 garlic cloves, finely chopped
2 handfuls of finely chopped
    coriander leaves
2 teaspoons dried mint
2 cardamom pods, bashed
1 teaspoon allspice
1 teaspoon ground cumin
½ teaspoon sumac
¼ teaspoon ground cinnamon
400g tin green lentils,
    drained and rinsed
1 tablespoon tomato purée
250ml vegetable stock
juice of ½ lemon
4 tablespoons pomegranate
    molasses
50g pomegranate seeds
20g walnuts, bashed
    into a fine rubble
sea salt

1. Cook the pasta in a large pan of boiling water for about 7–8 minutes until al dente. Drain and reserve 50ml of the pasta water.

2. Meanwhile, heat half the oil in a large pan over a medium heat. Add half the onions and cook, stirring occasionally, for 8–10 minutes until golden.

3. Put the garlic and half the coriander into the pan and mix well. Add the dried mint, cardamom, allspice, cumin, sumac and cinnamon. Season with a good pinch of salt and mix well.

4. Tip the cooked pasta and drained lentils into the pan with the onion and add the tomato purée, stock, lemon juice and pomegranate molasses. Mix together really well. Cover, reduce the heat to low and cook for 5–6 minutes or until the pasta is beautifully tender. Add the reserved pasta water to help slick up the sauce and mix well.

5. Meanwhile, heat the remaining oil in a small non-stick frying pan over a high heat and stir-fry the remaining onion for 6–8 minutes until really golden and crispy. Adjust the heat if the onion gets too dark too quickly.

6. Divide the pasta mixture between four serving bowls and garnish each one with pomegranate seeds, walnuts, fried onions and the remaining coriander. Drizzle each bowl with a little olive oil and serve immediately.

ROASTS & GRILLS

RITA'S BEEF SHAWARMA

Shawarma is a marinated meat dish that is popular throughout the Middle East. In Lebanon, chicken or lamb shawarma is found sizzling on bustling street corners across the country. In the mountain town of Jezzine, surrounded by lush pine forests, colourful wild flowers and a spectacular waterfall that cuts through the houses and tumbles into the valley below, I discovered a fabulous home-cooked version. The essence of the dish was still there, but it was tempered to be more homely.

SERVES 4

For the shawarma
6 garlic cloves
1 tablespoon fresh thyme leaves
1 tablespoon apple cider vinegar
100ml red wine
½ teaspoon allspice
5 tablespoons olive oil
3 sirloin steaks (about 220g each), fat trimmed and thinly sliced
2 onions, thinly sliced
350g tomatoes, finely chopped
1 tablespoon tomato purée
juice of ½ lemon
Buttery Noodle Rice to serve (page 149)
sea salt and freshly ground black pepper

For the tarator sauce
80g tahini
juice of ½ lemon
sea salt

For the onion
1 red onion, thinly sliced
juice of 1 lemon
a small handful of finely chopped parsley leaves
1½ teaspoons sumac
sea salt

1. Bash the garlic with a little salt into a paste. Add the thyme and bash again. Add the vinegar, wine, allspice, 2 tablespoons of the olive oil and a good pinch of pepper. Stir together and tip into a mixing bowl. Add the beef and mix together really well. Cover and leave to marinate overnight in the fridge.

2. The following day, heat the remaining oil in a large, shallow pan over a medium heat. Add the onions and cook, stirring occasionally, for 8–10 minutes until soft. Tip in the tomatoes and season with salt and pepper. Mix well and stir-fry for 4–5 minutes until the tomatoes have broken down. Add the tomato purée and mix well.

3. Tip the beef into the pan. Swirl 200ml of just-boiled water into the marinating dish to get all the flavour out and pour over the beef. Mix well and bring to the boil. Cover, reduce the heat to low and cook for 25–30 minutes until just cooked through and tender. Add the lemon juice and mix well. Check the seasoning. Increase the heat to medium and cook for 7–8 minutes for the sauce to thicken. Shake the pan occasionally to keep the beef submerged in the sauce. Once lovely and thick, turn off the heat. Cover and leave to rest for 5 minutes before eating.

4. Meanwhile, make the tarator sauce by whisking all the ingredients together with 65ml water until lovely and glossy.

5. Mix the onions with the lemon juice and a good pinch of salt. Leave to macerate for 15 minutes. Add the parsley and sumac and mix together.

6. To serve, divide the beef between four bowls full of Buttery Noodle Rice. Drizzle tarator sauce over the top and put some of the onions in the corner of each bowl. Serve immediately.

HOLE-IN-THE-WALL BEEF SKEWERS

Wander through the medina of Tripoli and you will soon smell the sizzle of beef kebabs wafting through the air as little hole-in-the-wall stalls grill up a storm throughout the day. To get the meat super succulent you need to have a high fat content – I suggest at least 20 per cent fat. These kebabs are simple to make and cook fast on a barbecue. Rather than serve them in a wrap, I like to make these a little different, plating them up on a slick of hummus – either buy your favourite or make a batch – and then top the meat with a really zesty mix of red onion, sumac and parsley.

SERVES 4

For the onion
1 red onion, finely sliced
juice of 1 lemon
1 teaspoon sumac
a small handful of finely
    chopped parsley leaves
sea salt

For the kebabs
450g minced beef with
    20 per cent fat
½ onion, grated
½ teaspoon allspice
a small handful of finely
    chopped parsley leaves
½ teaspoon Lebanese 7 spice
    or baharat
1½ teaspoons Aleppo
    pepper flakes
25g toasted pine nuts
2 garlic cloves, crushed

To serve
300g hummus
flatbreads

1. Put the sliced onion into a bowl and add the lemon juice and a good pinch of salt. Mix well and leave to macerate for 15 minutes.

2. Meanwhile, preheat the grill or barbecue to high. Put all the ingredients for the kebabs into a large mixing bowl with a good pinch of salt and mix well. Thread the meat onto flat skewers (these prevent the meat from turning when you flip them over on the barbecue) so you have a sausage shape. You should be able to make eight kebabs. Cook for 3–4 minutes on each side until charred and juicy.

3. Add the sumac and parsley to the macerated onions and mix well.

4. To serve, spread the hummus onto a serving dish. Lay the kebabs on top and pile on the onions. Serve immediately with flatbreads.

LAZY LAMB SKEWERS

Sunday barbecue with the family is a big deal in the mountains. It's the perfect time for everyone to come together and enjoy a feast. I was lucky enough to be invited to a Sunday gathering with Hodder and Charbel Naharoor at their beautiful farm perched right on the edge of the mountain, overlooking The Monastery of St Anthony of Qozhaya in Qadisha. It was wonderful. Three generations of the family sat together tucking into salads, freshly cooked breads, hummus, creamy labna, tabouleh and the most succulent lamb kebabs. The conversation flowed, as did the whisky, generously, and, much to my amusement, *Pitch Perfect* 2 was playing in the background the whole time. I come from a huge family and miss them desperately when I'm away, so it was a treat to be taken under the wing of such a friendly bunch. Food and family – you can't beat them.

SERVES 4

2 tablespoons olive oil
1 teaspoon dried oregano
½ teaspoon allspice
600g lamb leg, cut into
   2.5cm cubes
lemon wedges, to serve
sea salt

1. Put the olive oil into a mixing bowl and add the oregano, allspice and a good pinch of salt. Mix well. Add the lamb and mix together really well. Leave to marinate for at least 1 hour or overnight.

2. Preheat the grill or barbecue to high. Thread the lamb onto skewers. Remember, if you are using wooden skewers, to soak them for at least 10 minutes in cold water to stop them from burning. Grill for 2–3 minutes on two sides until charred and tender and just cooked through. Serve immediately with lemon wedges.

ALEPPO SOUR CHERRY KEBAB

[KABAB B'IL KARAZ]

This is the signature dish of Aleppo in Syria. Situated on the Silk Road, used by merchants for centuries, the city has a unique cooking style, heavy with spice, and Aleppans are not afraid to add fruit to savoury dishes. The sour cherries used for this dish are hard to find but worth every minute spent looking for them – get down to a Middle Eastern store near you and ask when they will get them in stock. They have a tart fragrance unlike anything else, and when they are cooked with a gesture of sugar and a hint of spice, the flavour develops into something incredibly complex. My friend Jonny taught me how to make her version in the pretty little village of Ammiq in the Beqaa Valley, just a stone's throw from the Syrian border.

SERVES 4

For the sour cherry sauce
350g pitted sour cherries
5 teaspoons caster sugar
a pinch (⅛ teaspoon)
    ground cinnamon
2 teaspoons pomegranate
    molasses
sea salt

For the kofta
600g minced lamb with
    20 per cent fat
¾ teaspoon allspice
¼ teaspoon ground cinnamon
3 tablespoons olive oil
sea salt and freshly ground
    black pepper

To garnish
25g toasted cashew nuts
a small handful of
    coriander leaves

1. To make the sour cherry sauce, put all the ingredients into a small pan with a little pinch of salt. Heat over a medium heat, stirring occasionally, until bubbling. Continue to cook, stirring occasionally, for 30–35 minutes until the cherries have broken down into a thick sauce but still have some texture. You might have to lower the heat a little if the sauce bubbles fiercely. Remove from the heat and set aside. If the sauce thickens too much while it stands, just mix in a splash of water.

2. Meanwhile, put the lamb into a mixing bowl and add the allspice, cinnamon and a good pinch of salt and pepper. Mix well and roll into walnut-sized balls. You should get about 20.

3. Heat the oil in a large, non-stick pan over a medium heat. Add the meatballs and cook for 4–5 minutes until golden on one side. Turn the meatballs over and lower the heat a little. Cook for 10–12 minutes, shaking the pan occasionally to roll the meatballs around, until just cooked through and golden. Drain off any excess oil.

4. Pour the cherry sauce into the pan with the meatballs and bring to the boil, shaking the pan to cover all the meatballs in the sauce. Check the seasoning. Transfer to a warm serving dish and garnish with the cashew nuts and coriander. Serve immediately.

KIBBEH WITH ONION
[KIBBEH BASA]

Without doubt, *kibbeh* is the national dish of Lebanon. It comes in many different varieties, all with a base of very fine-ground lamb and bulgur wheat. To understand such a dish I needed the best teacher, so I went to work with Lebanon's *kibbeh* queen, Georgina Bayeh. She lives in the pretty village of Zgharta near Tripoli in the north of the country. She took me through different versions of *kibbeh*, starting with her incredible *kibbeh* with onions. It's hard to replicate this dish perfectly as the lamb she used was farm fresh and minced so many times it was almost whipped. But my recipe is just as delicious and I love to serve it with yogurt, lemon wedges and a crisp side salad.

SERVES 4

70g extra fine bulgur
4 tablespoons olive oil
2 onions, finely sliced
1½ teaspoons allspice
15g toasted pine nuts
260g minced lamb
    with 5 per cent fat
sea salt

To *serve*
a small handful of finely
    chopped mint leaves
200g Greek yogurt
lemon wedges

1. Put the bulgur into a mixing bowl. Add some cold water and mix well. Drain and repeat several times to wash out the starch. Drain and then squeeze out any excess moisture with your hands.

2. Heat 3 tablespoons of the oil in a frying pan over a medium heat. Add the onions and cook, stirring occasionally, for 8–10 minutes until soft. Season with ½ teaspoon of the allspice and a good pinch of salt. Mix well. Tip into a round 23cm cake tin, spread out into an even layer and scatter over the pine nuts.

3. Preheat the oven to 200°C/180°C fan/gas mark 6. Tip the lamb into a blender and season with a really good pinch of salt. Add the remaining allspice and then blend for a couple of minutes until the meat is super fine. Add the bulgur and 55ml of water. Continue to blend until the bulgur is completely incorporated into the lamb. It should be a little sticky.

4. Run your hands under cold water to stop them sticking and then take a small piece of the lamb. Flatten it out between your hands until the meat is about 5mm thick. Place it over the onions. Repeat until the onions are completely covered. Wet your hands again and then smooth over the lamb, patting it down so you have a nice even layer of meat. Run a butter knife around the side of the dish to stop it sticking in the oven and wipe any excess meat from the sides of the tin.

5. Using a knife, score diagonal lines across the top of the kibbeh into a diamond pattern. Brush with the remaining olive oil and roast for 20–25 minutes or until just a little golden on the top. Remove from the oven and leave to cool. Cut into the diamond shapes you made and flip the kibbeh out onto a serving dish. Scatter over mint leaves and any pine nuts that are left in the pan. Serve with yogurt and lemon wedges.

KEBAB KING CHICKEN SHAWARMA

I am a man who likes routine and on arrival to Beirut I have a very set agenda: head to my rented apartment in Mar Mikhaël – I always choose one in this neighbourhood, it's so fun – and then walk down the road to Makhlouf, a tiny kebab shop in the Armenian neighbourhood Bourj Hammoud, for the best chicken shawarma in the world. The meat, which is one of those slightly mad-looking bulbous things spinning in the shop front, is so well spiced and juicy. It's wrapped up with masses of garlic sauce, chilli, salad and pickles. But the best bit is the chips. I mean, chips in a wrap. Double carbs. So wrong it's right. They are kept warm in a tray under the chicken, soaking up all the meaty juices and adding the most amazing flavour to the shawarma. For my version, I roast the chips together with the chicken and then get wrapping. If you can't find Lebanese garlic sauce, just mix a little mashed garlic with mayonnaise.

SERVES 4

For the marinade
1 teaspoon ground cumin
½ teaspoon ground coriander
½ teaspoon Lebanese 7 spice
  or baharat
½ teaspoon paprika
¼ teaspoon turmeric
1½ teaspoons cider vinegar
1 tablespoon olive oil
4 garlic cloves, crushed
55g Greek yogurt
sea salt and freshly ground
  black pepper

For the kebab
500g skinless, boneless
  chicken thigh fillets
300g potatoes, peeled
  and cut into chips
1 tablespoon olive oil
juice of ½ lemon
sea salt

To serve
Lebanese garlic sauce
4 large flatbreads
2 Baby Gem lettuce, shredded
2 large handfuls of parsley leaves
gherkins and pickled turnips,
  sliced
chilli sauce

1. Mix all the ingredients for the marinade together in a large mixing bowl along with a good pinch of salt and pepper. Add the chicken and mix well. Cover and refrigerate overnight.

2. The following day, when you are ready to cook, preheat the oven to 220°C/200°C fan/gas mark 7. Put the chips into a mixing bowl. Cover with cold water and soak for 5 minutes. Drain and pat dry with kitchen paper. Transfer to a roasting tray. Drizzle over the olive oil and season with salt. Mix well and roast for 12 minutes so that the chips start to soften.

3. Remove the chicken from the fridge and lay the fillets on a grilling rack. Remove the chips from the oven and turn. Place the grilling rack with the chicken over the tray of chips and return to the oven. Cook for 18–20 minutes or until the chicken is cooked through and beautifully tender. Slice the chicken into thin strips and squeeze over the lemon juice. Toss together.

4. To serve, spread loads of the garlic sauce over the flatbreads. Top with the lettuce, parsley, gherkins, pickled turnips, chicken and those incredibly soggy chips. Drizzle over chilli sauce to taste, roll up and devour.

FADIA'S CHICKEN FATTEH

Chicken *fatteh* is a decadent dish that is traditionally cooked during Ramadan for a feast. This particular version is my friend Fadia's recipe. She is a fabulous woman who lives in a stunning modern apartment in the rather beautiful coastal city of Jounieh. Designer shades clamped firmly to her head, she cooked me this incredible recipe. It's all about the layers of ingredients; rice, succulent shredded chicken and a creamy tarator sauce that coats everything.

SERVES 6 AS A HUGE MEAL WITH SALADS

1 free-range chicken (about 1.5kg)
1 cinnamon stick
   (about 10cm long)
4 bay leaves
4 onions, 2 halved and
   2 finely chopped
3 tablespoons olive oil
4 garlic cloves, finely sliced
large bunch of finely chopped
   coriander leaves and stalks
2 teaspoons Lebanese 7 spice
   or baharat, plus a pinch
   for garnish
300g Basmati rice
400g tin of chickpeas,
   rinsed and drained
juice of ½ lemon
sea salt

For the tarator sauce
220g Greek yogurt
200g tahini
juice of ½ lemon

To garnish
35g toasted almond flakes
40g pomegranate seeds

1. Put the chicken into a casserole and cover with about 2–2.5 litres of water. Add the cinnamon, bay leaves and halved onions. Bring to the boil over a high heat. Cover, reduce the heat to medium–low and cook for 1½–2 hours or until cooked through. Remove the chicken and leave to cool. Discard the skin and bones and shred the meat. Strain the stock and reserve for later.

2. Heat the oil in a pan over a medium heat and add the chopped onions. Cook for 10–12 minutes, stirring occasionally, until golden. Add the garlic and stir-fry for 10 seconds until fragrant. Add all but a handful of the coriander and the 7 spice. Mix well and add the rice. Pour over 600ml of the chicken stock and stir together once. Bring to the boil, cover, reduce the heat to low and cook for 10–12 minutes or until all the stock has been absorbed by the rice. Remove from the heat and tip in the chickpeas. Cover and leave for 4–5 minutes so that the chickpeas can warm through. Season with a good pinch of salt and add the lemon juice. Fork together.

3. To make the sauce, put the yogurt, tahini, 50ml water and the lemon juice into a small saucepan. Mix well and warm through over a low heat, stirring occasionally, for 4–5 minutes. If it gets too thick, just add a little more water and mix well.

4. When you're ready to eat, tip the rice onto a serving dish and scatter over the shredded chicken. Drizzle a little of the tarator sauce over the top and garnish with the almond flakes, pomegranate seeds and remaining coriander. Add a pinch of Lebanese 7 spice and serve immediately with the remaining sauce in a bowl.

SUMAC & SEVEN-SPICE ROAST CHICKEN

I come from a long line of chicken lovers. As kids we consumed so much of the stuff it's a wonder that we never started clucking at each other. My mum would cook chicken in different guises from roasted to grilled and curried to stewed. It was a mid-week meal, a weekend feast or a sensational sandwich to snack on. Over the years I have dined on grilled chicken from all over the world and this recipe from the rich farming region of the Beqaa Valley is rocking. The marinade tenderises the meat and gives it an incredible depth of flavour. You can roast or barbecue the chicken and every time it comes out perfectly. Serve with Classic Fattoush (page 21) and a side of Coriander, Garlic & Chilli Potato Wedges (page 25) and you have one of the best meals around.

SERVES 4

For the marinade
5 garlic cloves, peeled
2 tablespoons olive oil
2 teaspoons Lebanese 7 spice
  or baharat
2 teaspoons dried oregano
1 teaspoon paprika
1 teaspoon sumac
½ teaspoon ground cinnamon
2 cardamom pods, bashed
juice of 1 lemon
sea salt

For the chicken
1kg chicken thighs and legs,
  skin on
2 tablespoons olive oil
¼ teaspoon paprika
juice of ½ lemon
2 teaspoons za'atar
sea salt

1. To make the marinade, bash the garlic into a paste with a little salt. Tip into a large bowl and add the olive oil, Lebanese 7 spice, oregano, paprika, sumac, cinnamon, cardamom and lemon juice. Mix well. Add the chicken and toss together to coat the meat completely in the marinade. Cover and refrigerate for 3 hours or overnight if you are organised.

2. When you are ready to cook, preheat the oven to 220°C/200°C fan/ gas mark 7 and tip the chicken into a baking tray. Brush with the olive oil and sprinkle over the paprika. Roast for 40–45 minutes, turning halfway, until cooked through and tender. Transfer to a serving dish and squeeze over the lemon juice. Scatter over the za'atar and a good pinch of salt. Serve immediately.

THE ULTIMATE SHISH TAOUK

Almost certainly of Ottoman origin, shish is taken from the Turkish word şiş, meaning skewer. Traditionally for this style of kebab, the meat is threaded onto long, flat metal skewers that lie directly over the hot coals. Because they're flat, the meat doesn't roll around when you turn the skewers as you cook. This garlicky chicken kebab is synonymous with barbecue all over Lebanon and the Middle East. The mix of yogurt and lemon tenderises the chicken so it remains succulent and juicy on the inside and charred and smoky on the outside. Spices – of which there are endless combinations – inject further flavour into the meat. The traditional way to serve a shish taouk in Lebanon is in a flatbread with masses of chilli sauce, salad and pickles.

SERVES 4

For the marinade
4 garlic cloves
80g Greek yogurt
1 teaspoon ground cumin
½ teaspoon ground coriander
½ teaspoon Lebanese 7 spice
    or baharat
sea salt

600g skinless, boneless
    chicken thigh fillets,
    cut into 5cm chunks
1 red onion, finely sliced
juice of 1 lemon
½ teaspoon sumac
sea salt

To serve
200g Labna (see page 24)
4 large flatbreads
bunch of parsley leaves
chilli sauce

1. To make the marinade, bash the garlic into a paste with a little salt. Put it in a large mixing bowl and add the yogurt, cumin, coriander and 7 spice. Mix everything together really well. Add the chicken to the bowl and toss together so that you get a lovely coating of marinade on all the chunks of meat. Cover and refrigerate overnight.

2. Preheat the grill or barbecue to high. Thread the chicken onto four skewers. If you are using wooden skewers, remember to soak them for at least 10 minutes in cold water to stop them from burning. Grill for 4–5 minutes on two sides until charred and tender and just cooked through.

3. Meanwhile, put the sliced onion into a bowl and squeeze over the lemon. Add the sumac and a good pinch of salt. Mix well and leave to macerate for at least 15 minutes.

4. To serve, spread the labna over the flatbreads and divide the parsley between them. Take the meat off the skewers and arrange in a line over the parsley. Top with the onions and load on chilli sauce to taste. Wrap up and enjoy.

SAFFRON-SCENTED CHRISTMAS CHICKEN

When I first went to visit my wonderful friend Rita, who lives in the tiny hamlet of Bteddine just outside Jezzine south of Beirut, it was Easter. Her lovely house was decked out with gaudy bunnies and brightly painted eggs. I was there to learn about the local food of this mountainous region and she took me through so many mouth-watering classics. She decided to pull out all the stops and cook me a celebratory dish that was usually her family's favourite Christmas dinner – *dik saghir* or cockerel, in reference to the glorious stuffed bird that forms the centrepiece of this sharing platter.

SERVES 4–6

4 tablespoons olive oil
200g finely minced lamb
    with 20 per cent fat
30g pine nuts
200g Basmati rice
¾ teaspoon allspice
¼ teaspoon ground cinnamon
1050ml chicken stock
1 free-range chicken (about 1.5kg)
2 onions, halved
1 tomato, quartered
a head of garlic, halved
1 cinnamon stick (about 10cm)
4 bay leaves
pinch of saffron strands
20g butter
sea salt

To *garnish*
35g cashew nuts
20g flaked almonds
30g sultanas
a small handful of finely
    chopped parsley leaves

1. Heat half the olive oil in a large, non-stick frying pan over a high heat. Add the lamb and stir-fry for 4–5 minutes until just cooked. Add half the pine nuts and stir-fry for a further minute until golden. Add the rice, allspice, cinnamon and a pinch of salt and mix well. Pour in 300ml of the stock and stir together. Cover, reduce the heat to low and cook for 8–10 minutes until the rice has absorbed the stock but still has a little bite.

2. Preheat the oven to 200°C/180°C fan/gas mark 6. Use half the rice to stuff the chicken, spooning the rice into the cavity and pushing it in until full. Tie the legs together to hold in the rice.

3. Pour the remaining oil into a lidded casserole that will snugly fit the chicken. Place the chicken in the dish and add the onions, tomato, garlic, cinnamon and bay leaves. Pour in the remaining 750ml of stock, which should be enough to come just under halfway up the chicken. Cover and roast for 1½ hours or until the chicken is cooked through and the juices run clear. Remove from the oven and spoon the sauce over the top. Return to the oven uncovered for 20–30 minutes or until the chicken skin is a little golden. Transfer to a warm plate. Cover with foil and leave to rest. Strain the stock and skim off any fat.

4. Mix 120ml of the stock from the chicken pot into the frying pan with the remaining rice. Bring to the boil over a high heat. Cover, reduce the heat to low and cook for 12–15 minutes or until the rice has absorbed all the liquid. Season well.

5. Meanwhile, pour the remaining stock from the chicken pot into a saucepan and bring to the boil over a high heat. Add the saffron and mix well. Reduce the heat to medium and simmer, stirring occasionally, for 18–20 minutes or until reduced by two-thirds. Turn off the heat and whisk in the butter. Pour into a serving jug.

6. To serve, tip the rice onto a serving dish and put the chicken next to it. Garnish with the cashew nuts, almonds, sultanas, parsley and the remaining pine nuts. Serve immediately with the sauce.

CHARRED OCTOPUS WITH TOMATOES & OREGANO

One of my favourite restaurants in Beirut is Baron, where modern Lebanese food is served in an industrial dining room, softened by marble-topped tables and rustic wooden chairs. They mash up old favourites and drop in soon-to-be new classics. I often treat myself to a dinner at the counter where I watch the chefs work their magic. This recipe is inspired by their delicious dish of charred octopus served with vibrant cherry tomatoes that have been left to relax in a warm dressing so they are literally bursting open with flavour. It's bright and breezy coastal food with a very modern edge. I use shop-bought cooked octopus, but you can prepare and cook it yourself if you like.

SERVES 2 AS A LIGHT LUNCH OR 4 AS AN APPETISER

4 tablespoons olive oil
2 garlic cloves, finely chopped
½ red chilli, finely chopped
300g red and yellow baby
    tomatoes, halved
juice of 1 lemon
a large handful of fresh
    oregano leaves
4 small cooked octopus
    tentacles (about 450g)
2 large handfuls of parsley leaves
a large handful of roughly
    chopped mint leaves
½ teaspoon sumac, to serve
sea salt

1. Heat 3 tablespoons of the olive oil in a frying pan over a medium heat. Add the garlic, chilli and tomatoes. Season with a good pinch of salt. Mix well and cook, stirring occasionally, for 2–3 minutes until the tomatoes relax a little in the oil. Add half the lemon juice and most of the oregano. Mix well and remove from the heat. Set to one side to cool down for a few minutes while you cook the octopus.

2. Heat a griddle pan over a high heat or preheat the barbecue to high. Wash the octopus thoroughly, pat dry and tip into a mixing bowl. Pour the remaining oil over the top and season with salt. Toss together. Griddle or barbecue for 2–3 minutes a side until the tentacles have a few griddle lines and are crispy.

3. Tip the tomatoes and all the juices into a mixing bowl. Add the parsley, mint, remaining lemon juice and a pinch of salt. Toss together and tip onto two serving plates. Top with the octopus and scatter over the sumac and remaining oregano leaves. Serve immediately.

MAGUY'S CHILLI & MINT PRAWNS

My friend Maguy has a wonderful family-run seafood restaurant on a picturesque beach in Batroun between Beirut and Tripoli. Chez Maguy has the best location; to one side the ancient Phoenician port wall still stands and to the other, crystal clear waters gently lap the dining terrace. A well-positioned ladder leads straight into the sea for the ultimate after-dinner dip. Maguy cooks everything at a million miles an hour on a barbecue, including these perfect prawns that she tosses into a frying pan, hot from the coals, to keep all the juices for dunking.

SERVES 2 AS A MAIN OR 4 AS PART OF A MEAL

5 tablespoons olive oil
4 garlic cloves, finely chopped
4 spring onions, finely chopped
½ red chilli, finely chopped
350g raw giant king prawns, heads and tails on
a handful of finely chopped mint leaves
¼ teaspoon allspice
sea salt

1. Heat the olive oil in a frying pan over a high heat. Add the garlic, spring onions and chilli and stir-fry for 1 minute until fragrant. Chuck in the prawns and a good pinch of salt. Cook the prawns for 1–1½ minutes a side, shaking the pan so that the other ingredients don't burn, until the prawns are coral pink and cooked through.

2. Scatter the mint and allspice into the pan and mix well. Tip the prawns and all the lovely juices onto a serving dish and serve immediately.

SUNSET SCALLOPS

A visit to see my friend Maguy in Batroun is always eventful. One minute we're driving around town at breakneck speed in a 'Karma Cab' blasting out old Lebanese pop songs and the next we're toasting glasses of cold raki over an opulent seafood spread next to the sea. One of her signature dishes is scallops grilled on the barbecue with a mix of sumac, garlic and mint. Cooking them in the shells is wonderful. They hold all the buttery juices so you can eat the scallops and then dunk bread in afterwards to mop up the sauce.

SERVES 4 AS A STARTER

120g soft butter
4 garlic cloves, crushed
2 handfuls of finely chopped mint
    leaves, plus extra to garnish
3 teaspoons sumac,
    plus extra to garnish
½ teaspoon Aleppo pepper flakes
12 large scallops and their shells
juice of ½ lemon
sea salt

1. Mix together the butter, garlic, mint, sumac, Aleppo pepper flakes and a good pinch of salt in a mixing bowl.

2. Preheat the barbecue to high. Divide the butter between the scallop shells and place onto the barbecue. Once the butter has melted, add the scallops and cook for 1–2 minutes a side until just cooked through and super tender. The shells get really hot so use a good pair of tongs to take them off the barbecue.

3. Squeeze a little lemon over each scallop and add a tiny pinch of sumac and some mint leaves. Serve immediately.

SPICY TAHINI SEA BASS
[SAMKE HARRA]

Originating in Tripoli, *samke harra* or 'spicy fish' is simple baked seafood served with a rich tahini sauce spiked with garlic, chilli and coriander. It's a comfort classic, the kind of food you want waiting for you on a cold night after a long day at work. Housewives up and down the country have their own recipe. In the incredible old town of El Mina in Tripoli, you can find a street food version made to an age-old recipe at Abou Fadi's hole-in-the-wall restaurant Malak El Samke Harra, which translates as 'King of Spicy Fish'. I like to serve mine at the table with whole seabass, but you can just as easily skin and bone the fish before serving with the sauce.

SERVES 2 AS A MAIN OR 4 AS PART OF A MEAL

For the sea bass
4 garlic cloves, peeled
a large handful of finely
    chopped coriander leaves
1 teaspoon ground coriander
½ teaspoon ground cumin
½ teaspoon Aleppo pepper flakes
3 tablespoons olive oil
juice of ½ lemon
2 farmed sea bass (about 800g)
    gutted, cleaned and scaled
sea salt

For the sauce
120g tahini
juice of 1½ lemons
2 tablespoons olive oil
1 onion, thinly sliced
3 garlic cloves, crushed
½ teaspoon ground cumin
½ teaspoon ground coriander
1 teaspoon Aleppo pepper flakes
sea salt

To garnish
a small handful of coriander
    leaves
15g toasted flaked almonds

1. Preheat the oven to 200°C/180°C fan/gas mark 6. Bash the garlic for the sea bass into a paste with a little salt. Add the coriander leaves and bash together. Add the ground coriander, cumin, Aleppo pepper flakes, olive oil, lemon juice and a little more salt and stir together. Cut a few slits into the flesh on both sides of each sea bass. Rub the marinade all over the fish, inside and out. Place in a roasting dish and roast for 20–25 minutes until just cooked through.

2. Meanwhile, mix together the tahini, lemon juice, 150ml of water and a good pinch of salt into a smooth sauce.

3. Heat the olive oil in a frying pan over a medium heat. Add the onion and cook, stirring occasionally, for 8–10 minutes until golden. Add the garlic, cumin, ground coriander and Aleppo pepper flakes. Mix well. Pour over the tahini sauce and stir together. Heat for 1–2 minutes, stirring continuously, until warmed through. Remove from the heat and check the salt.

4. Place the sea bass on warm serving plates and spoon over the lovely juices left in the roasting dish.

5. Add a few tablespoons of water to the tahini sauce. As you mix it in, it will bring it back into a really silky, shiny sauce. Spoon over the bass and garnish with the coriander and almonds. Serve immediately.

MACKEREL MÉCHOUI

Méchoui is Arabic for 'roasted' or 'grilled', and in this case it describes a stunning grilled fish inspired by my time in Beqaa Valley. The valley tears down through the east of Lebanon. It's their wine country and the border to neighbouring Syria. During a weekend feast at Beit Ammiq, a beautiful restaurant that supports the local community with jobs and a place to sell farm foods, I barbecued whole sumac-spiked river fish with one of their chefs. We sat on the terrace tucking into the fish for lunch, the hazy valley stretching out in front of us and on to the snow-capped mountains in Syria. It was extraordinary being somewhere so peaceful and enjoying such fabulous hospitality. In that moment, I would never have thought that I was next to one of the most volatile places on earth. But I came to realise that this is one of the reasons why there is so much spirit and energy in Lebanon – with the country's history and proximity to conflict, its people know how precious life is and commit to living it to the fullest.

SERVES 4

For the marinade
4 garlic cloves
bunch of finely chopped
    coriander leaves and stalks
2 teaspoons paprika
juice of 2 lemons
4 tablespoons olive oil
½ red chilli
25g tahini
30g walnuts
sea salt

4 mackerel (about 280g each),
    gutted, cleaned and scaled

For the dipping sauce
2 garlic cloves, crushed
juice of 2½ lemons
2 teaspoons sumac
1 red onion, finely chopped
1 handful of finely chopped
    parsley leaves
sea salt

1. Put all the ingredients for the marinade into a food-processor with 30ml water and a good pinch of salt. Blend until lovely and smooth. Put the mackerel into a dish and pour over the marinade. Rub it inside and out so the fish are completely covered. Cover and marinate for 30 minutes in the fridge.

2. Meanwhile, make the dipping sauce. Mix the garlic, lemon, sumac and red onion together with a good pinch of salt. Leave for the flavours to develop whilst you cook the fish.

3. Preheat the barbecue or grill to high and grill the mackerel for 5–6 minutes each side or until charred on the outside and cooked through. Transfer to a serving dish.

4. Mix the parsley into the dipping sauce. Spoon some of the sauce over the cooked fish and serve immediately with the rest in a bowl.

ROCK STAR ROASTED CAULIFLOWER

Cauliflower was always such a wrong 'un when I was growing up, too often boiled and battered into an unpleasant mess. How did we get it so wrong, when in the Middle East they were roasting it, charring the outside and concentrating the flavour? Thank God this is now common knowledge and the modest brassica is back in vogue. In Lebanon, roasted cauliflower makes a regular appearance on a banquet table, and during the preparations for a feast in Ammiq in Beqaa Valley, my friend Salima cooked a local version of the dish that started with a base of green peppers and onions mixed with tahini, the tradition of her little village. She topped this with roasted cauliflower and garnished it with nuts and herbs. It was sublime, catapulting the humble veg to rock-star status. Unlike the usual green bell pepper, Lebanese green peppers have a sweet note, so in this recipe I have swapped them for the more palatable red pepper to get the flavours right.

SERVES 4

1 cauliflower, cut into florets,
   any baby leaves reserved
4 tablespoons olive oil,
   plus extra for drizzling
1 red onion, finely sliced
1 red pepper, deseeded
   and finely sliced
80g tahini
juice of ½ lemon
sea salt and freshly ground
   black pepper

To garnish
a small handful of finely
   chopped coriander leaves
½ teaspoon sumac
½ teaspoon Aleppo pepper flakes
15g toasted pine nuts

1. Preheat the oven to 220°C/200°C fan/gas mark 7 and put the cauliflower florets and leaves onto a roasting tray. Pour over 2 tablespoons of the olive oil and season with salt and pepper. Toss together and cook for 30–35 minutes or until charred and tender.

2. Heat the remaining oil in a large frying pan over a medium heat and add the onion and red pepper. Season with salt and black pepper and mix well. Cook, stirring occasionally, for 12–15 minutes until golden, adding a splash of water after about 6–8 minutes to help soften the pepper. Remove from the heat.

3. Meanwhile, mix the tahini with 65ml of water, the lemon juice and a good pinch of salt into a smooth sauce. Pour over the cooked pepper and onion. Mix everything together really well and add more salt to taste. Heat over a medium heat for a few minutes to warm the sauce through. Add a little more water if the sauce starts to split – it will bring it back together in an instant.

4. To serve, spoon the cooked sauce onto a serving dish. Top with the cauliflower florets and leaves. Garnish with coriander, sumac, Aleppo pepper flakes and pine nuts. Drizzle over a little more oil and serve immediately.

STEWS

BEIRUTI MEATBALLS
[DAOUT BASHA]

My friend Rima Khodr is one of the coolest ladies I have come across, so full of life and energy –
and boy, can she cook. We spent the day together and she taught me how to make her Beiruti
meatballs. She explained to me that this recipe was named after an Ottoman man called Daout
Basha. I have slightly adapted her recipe, adding tomatoes to the sauce to make it a little richer, but
kept that classic Lebanese tartness running through it with pomegranate molasses and lemon juice.

SERVES 4

For the sauce
2 tablespoons olive oil
1½ onions, finely sliced
4 garlic cloves, finely chopped
4 tomatoes, finely chopped
2 tablespoons tomato purée
½ teaspoon allspice
½ teaspoon ground cinnamon,
   plus extra to garnish
1 tablespoon pomegranate
   molasses
400ml chicken stock
1¼ teaspoons dried mint
½ teaspoon cornflour
10g butter
juice of ½ lemon

For the meatballs
500g beef mince with
   15–20 per cent fat
½ onion, grated
1 teaspoon allspice
½ teaspoon Lebanese 7 spice
   or baharat
¼ teaspoon ground cinnamon
a handful of finely chopped
   parsley leaves
sea salt

1. Heat the olive oil in a large pan over a medium heat. Add the
onions and cook, stirring occasionally, for 12–15 minutes until lovely
and golden. Add the garlic and mix well. Tip the tomatoes into the
pan and add the tomato purée and a good pinch of salt. Mix well and
cook, stirring occasionally, for 3–4 minutes so that the tomatoes start
to break down. Add the allspice, cinnamon, pomegranate molasses,
chicken stock and 1 teaspoon of the dried mint. Mix everything together
really well. Cover, reduce the heat to low and cook for 10–12 minutes
or until everything comes together into a lovely sauce.

2. Meanwhile, mix together all the ingredients for the meatballs in
a mixing bowl with a good pinch of salt, saving some of the parsley
for garnish. Roll into 16 walnut-sized meatballs.

3. Transfer the meatballs into the sauce and shake the pan so that
they settle. They should be about half covered. Bring to the boil, cover,
reduce the heat to low and cook for 10–12 minutes or until just cooked
through, turning the meatballs halfway..Take the meatballs out of
the sauce and let them rest on a warm serving dish.

4. Bring the sauce to the boil over a high heat. Cook, stirring
occasionally, for 6–8 minutes until lovely and thick.

5. Mash the cornflour into the butter and add it to the sauce with the
lemon juice. Whisk for 1–2 minutes to further thicken the sauce. Check
the seasoning and add salt to taste. Pour the sauce over the meatballs
and garnish with the remaining dried mint and a pinch of cinnamon.
Scatter over the reserved parsley. Serve immediately.

BEEF & BROAD BEANS IN YOGURT

[FESTQIYEH]

Springtime in Lebanon is pretty as a picture. The countryside is strewn with a vibrant carpet of pastel-coloured wild flowers and the air smells of za'atar, oregano and basil. All along the country roads, little stalls pop up selling fresh fava beans – broad beans as we know them. Dinner tables are adorned with great bowls of the verdant vegetable and hungry diners enjoy the beans raw as an appetiser. This simple stew is a celebration of these beans. They are cooked in a light yogurt sauce with a little beef shin for extra flavour. I have given instructions for using both fresh and frozen beans so you can make this delightful dish anytime.

SERVES 4

2 beef shin steaks
    (about 300g each)
2 onions, 1 halved and
    1 finely chopped
150g podded broad beans,
    fresh or frozen
2 tablespoons olive oil
2 garlic cloves, finely chopped
small bunch of finely chopped
    coriander leaves and stalks,
    plus a few leaves to garnish
juice of ½ lemon
350g full-fat Greek yogurt
sea salt

1. Put the beef into a casserole and add the halved onion. Pour over 850ml of just-boiled water and bring to the boil. Cover, reduce the heat to low and simmer gently for 3–3½ hours, skimming off any scum, or until the meat is so tender it falls apart at the touch of a fork. Remove from the pot and shred with two forks, picking out and discarding any fat. Pour 150ml of the stock created into a heatproof jug to use later when you make your sauce.

2. Meanwhile, cook the beans in a pan of boiling water until just tender. Frozen ones only take 1 minute and fresh 2–3 minutes. Drain, refresh under cold running water, then drain again.

3. Heat the olive oil in a large frying pan over a medium heat and add the chopped onion. Cook, stirring occasionally, for 5–6 minutes until just soft. Add the garlic and coriander and stir-fry for a minute until fragrant.

4. Pour the reserved stock into the pan with the onions and add the lemon juice. Mix well. Turn down the heat to low, scoop the yogurt into the sauce and add a good pinch of salt. Mix well – the sauce can split if you use low-fat yogurt, so go full-fat; it's much tastier. Once the yogurt has melted into the sauce, tip the beans into the pan and add the shredded meat. Mix everything together really well and serve immediately.

JEW'S MALLOW CHICKEN SOUP

Jew's mallow or *mulukhiyah* is a vegetable that is found in abundance during the spring and summer months in the mountains of Lebanon. The leaves have a very mellow, fresh flavour and they are typically used to make this light chicken soup. Like okra, *mulukhiyah* has a sticky quality and requires quite a lot of effort to prepare so it doesn't become gooey. The leaves are washed well and then dried out in the sun for a few hours, then shredded into a light chicken stock to cook. This is served DIY-style with bowls of rice, sliced chicken and macerated onions. Jew's mallow leaves are not very supermarket-friendly. Occasionally I have been able to find them frozen in Middle Eastern stores. For this recipe (purists look away now) I've substituted a mix of Swiss chard, spinach and spring greens, which I promise you is just as delicious.

SERVES 6

1 free-range chicken
(about 1.5kg)
2 onions, halved
1 stick cinnamon (about 10cm)
4 bay leaves
4 cardamom pods
300g Basmati rice
3 tablespoons olive oil
6 garlic cloves, finely chopped
a large bunch of finely chopped
coriander leaves and stalks
100g Swiss chard, stalks removed
and leaves finely sliced
100g baby spinach
100g spring greens,
stalks removed and leaves
finely sliced
juice of 2 lemons
1 red onion, finely sliced
sea salt and freshly ground
black pepper

1. Put the chicken into a large casserole with the onions, cinnamon, bay leaves and cardamom. Pour over 2.5 litres of water to just cover everything. Bring to the boil over a high heat. Cover, reduce the heat to medium–low and cook for 1½–2 hours until cooked through and tender. Remove the chicken and strain and reserve the stock. Once cool, shred the chicken, discarding the skin and bones. Place on a warm serving dish and cover.

2. Put the rice into a saucepan and pour over 600ml of the reserved chicken stock. Bring to the boil over a high heat. Cover, reduce the heat to low and cook for 10–12 minutes or until the water has been absorbed. Remove from the heat and leave to stand, covered, for 10 minutes to fluff up.

3. Meanwhile, heat the olive oil in a large pan over a medium heat. Add the garlic and coriander and stir-fry for about 1 minute until the herbs wilt and the garlic is fragrant. Add the chard, spinach and spring greens and stir-fry for 2–3 minutes until wilted. Season with a good pinch of salt and pepper and mix well.

4. Pour 1.4 litres of the reserved chicken stock into the pan with the greens. Bring to the boil over a high heat. Reduce the heat to low and simmer gently for 10 minutes to soften the greens. Add half the lemon juice and mix well. Check the seasoning, adding salt to taste.

5. Meanwhile, put the red onion into a serving bowl. Add the remaining lemon juice and a good pinch of salt. Mix well and leave to macerate for 15 minutes.

6. To serve, spoon the rice into bowls and top with the shredded chicken. Pour over plenty of the soup and serve immediately with the onions.

IRAQI LEMON KIBBEH
[KIBBEH BAR MOUNT]

In her gorgeous bougainvillea covered apartment in Jounieh, my friend Fadia taught me how to make this delicately flavoured dish, *kibbeh bar mount*. It's based on an old Iraqi recipe, which she has tweaked to suit a Lebanese palate. The name means '*kibbeh* with lemon', but instead of the typical bulgur and minced lamb *kibbeh* mix for the outer case of the dumplings, she uses rice, and it's cooked in a sauce. The result is quite different and the rice swells out of the dumplings when cooked, but it softens and absorbs all the flavour of the tomatoes, lemon and chard.

SERVES 4

100g Basmati rice
500g minced lamb with
   15–20 per cent fat
¾ teaspoon allspice
15g pine nuts
a small handful of finely
   chopped parsley leaves
2 tablespoons olive oil
1 onion, finely chopped
4 tomatoes, finely chopped
2 tablespoons tomato purée
juice of 1 lemon
200g Swiss chard, stalks
   discarded and leaves
   finely chopped
lemon wedges, to serve
sea salt

1. Start by making the outer case for the kibbeh. Tip the rice into a colander and wash until the water runs clear. Transfer to a food-processor and give a quick pulse to break the rice down a little. Add 300g of the lamb, ½ teaspoon of the allspice and a good pinch of salt. Continue to blend until completely mixed together. Take the mixture out of the food-processor and divide into 16 portions. Roll each one into a ball.

2. Next make the filling. Put the remaining lamb into a mixing bowl and add the pine nuts, parsley and remaining allspice. Season with a good pinch of salt and mix together really well. Divide into 16 portions and roll each into a ball.

3. Wet your hands a little to stop the mix sticking to them. Using your thumb, make a well in each portion of the outercase mix. Put a portion of the filling into the centre and close up the hole. Roll back into a ball and then gently flatten.

4. Heat the olive oil in a large saucepan over a medium heat. Add the onion and cook, stirring occasionally, for 6–8 minutes until golden. Tip the tomatoes into the pan and add a good pinch of salt. Mix well. Cook, stirring occasionally, for 3–4 minutes so that the tomatoes start to break down. Add the tomato purée, 200ml of just-boiled water and the lemon juice. Mix well and bring to the boil. Simmer for 5–6 minutes, stirring occasionally, until you have a lovely thick sauce.

5. Carefully put the kibbeh into the sauce. Pour over 150ml of just-boiled water. Cover, reduce the heat to low and cook for 10 minutes, then turn the kibbeh over in the sauce. Add the chard, cover the pan and cook for a further 8–10 minutes until the kibbeh are cooked through and the chard has wilted. Serve immediately with lemon wedges for squeezing over the top.

LEBANESE TORTELLINI

[SHISH BARAK]

This is one of those incredible ancient dishes that you can find in different guises all over the Levant. *Shish barak* are little meat-filled dumplings swimming in a yogurt sauce. They have a very distinct look, resembling little hats or ears, hence the name, which is thought to come from the Persian words *gosh e-barreh* or 'lamb's ear'. My *shish barak* are adapted from a recipe from the Mount Lebanon region. It's not uncommon to bake the dumplings until golden and then toss them straight into the yogurt sauce. I like the softer texture that comes from boiling, and an intense labna sauce.

SERVES 4

For the tortellini
200g plain flour, plus
 extra for dusting
4 tablespoons olive oil,
 plus extra for oiling
1 onion, finely chopped
250g minced lamb with
 10 per cent fat
½ teaspoon allspice
1 teaspoon dried mint
sea salt

For the sauce
400g labna (see page 42)
1 garlic clove, crushed
juice of ½ lemon
40g butter
1 teaspoon Aleppo pepper flakes

To garnish
20g toasted pine nuts
1 teaspoon sumac
a small handful of finely
 chopped mint leaves

1. Put the flour into a mixing bowl and add a pinch of salt. Mix well and pour in 125ml water. Bring together into a dough, then knead on a floured surface for 6–8 minutes until smooth. Place in an oiled bowl and leave to rest for 30 minutes.

2. Meanwhile, heat 2 tablespoons of the olive oil in a frying pan over a medium heat and add the onion and lamb. Cook, stirring occasionally, for 8–10 minutes until golden. Add the allspice, dried mint, a good pinch of salt and a few tablespoons of water to help bring everything together and mix well. Tip into a mixing bowl and leave to cool.

3. Divide the dough into 32 portions. Roll each one into a ball, then roll out into rounds about 8cm in diameter. Wet your finger and run it around the edge of one of the rounds. Place a teaspoon of the filling in the middle. Fold the circle in half over the filling and seal. Pull the two sides together and gently squeeze them so that they stick. Place on a baking sheet lined with baking paper. Repeat with the rest.

4. Bring a large pan of water to the boil over a high heat and pour in the remaining oil. Carefully add the tortellini, in batches, and cook for 2–3 minutes until fluffy. Drain and repeat with the rest.

5. To make the sauce, mix the labna in a small pan with the garlic, lemon juice, a good pinch of salt and 120–150ml of water into a smooth sauce. Stir over a low heat for 4–5 minutes until warmed through.

6. Melt the butter in a small pan over a medium heat. Add the Aleppo pepper flakes and a pinch of salt. Mix well and remove from the heat. Leave for 30 seconds to infuse.

7. To serve, swirl the yogurt sauce on four serving plates and top each one with eight of the dumplings. Drizzle over the vibrant red butter and garnish with the pine nuts, sumac and mint leaves. Serve immediately.

PALMYRA YOGURT SOUP

Baalbek is a dusty town in the foothills of Lebanon's mountainous interior, located in the Beqaa Valley slap bang between Beirut and Damascus. It's an old Roman city and on the outskirts the incredible temples of Jupiter, Venus and, most extraordinary of all, Bacchus still stand. The best views of the Temple of Bacchus are from the roof of the Palmyra Hotel. This accidentally Wes Anderson-style hotel, crammed with quirky artefacts, is curated by a wonderful woman called Rima Husseini, who is glamorous, kind and clever and passionate about Baalbek. On my last visit she prepared this warming winter soup for me made with *kishk* – dried fermented yogurt. The soup is typical of the region, using local lamb that is considered the best in Lebanon. I've replaced the *kishk* with labna to make it easier. It's just as hearty and reminds me of Rima and those fabulous ruins.

SERVES 2

2 tablespoons olive oil
200g potatoes, peeled
    and cut into 5mm cubes
1 onion, finely chopped
120g minced lamb with
    20 per cent fat
1 teaspoon allspice
300g Labna (see page 24)
sea salt

1. Heat the olive oil in a saucepan over a medium heat and add the potatoes. Cook, stirring occasionally, for 8–10 minutes until soft. Add the onion and lamb and a good pinch of salt. Mix well and cook, stirring occasionally, for 6–8 minutes until the onion is lovely and golden, and the lamb cooked through. Add the allspice and mix well.

2. Mix the labna with 200ml of cold water and pour into the pan with the lamb. Stir everything together really well. Reduce the heat to low and warm the labna through, stirring occasionally, for 5–6 minutes. Check the seasoning and add salt to taste. Divide between two bowls and serve immediately.

MUM'S OKRA YAKHNI

You can't beat the mid-week meals that your mum used to make when you were growing up. Those simple food-hug dishes that could make a bad day disappear. In Lebanon this would be *yakhni*, a sumptuous stew made from a combination of meat, vegetables and pulses, cooked in a tomato sauce and served with rice. Every mum has their own recipe, which, to her kids, is the best. This one, for okra *yakhni*, is rich and wonderfully comforting and was lovingly passed onto me by some friends from Jezzine, south of Beirut.

SERVES 4

6 tablespoons olive oil
600g lamb leg, cut into
   2.5cm cubes
1 onion, finely chopped
6 garlic cloves, crushed
a large handful of finely
   chopped coriander leaves
   and stalks, separated
4 tomatoes, finely chopped
2 tablespoons tomato purée
2 tablespoons pomegranate
   molasses
¾ teaspoon allspice
400ml lamb stock
350g okra, halved lengthways
30g walnuts
Buttery Noodle Rice,
   to serve (page 149)
sea salt

1. Heat 2 tablespoons of the olive oil in a casserole over a medium heat. Add the lamb and cook, stirring occasionally, for 8–10 minutes until brown on all sides. Add the onion, mix well and cook for 4–5 minutes until soft. Add five of the garlic cloves, all of the coriander stalks and half the leaves. Season with a good pinch of salt and mix well. Stir-fry for 30 seconds until fragrant.

2. Tip the tomatoes into the pan and cook, stirring occasionally, for 5–6 minutes until broken down. Add the tomato purée, 1 tablespoon of the pomegranate molasses, the allspice and the stock. Mix well. There should be enough liquid to just cover everything. Bring to the boil, cover and reduce the heat to low. Cook for 1 hour or until the lamb is tender.

3. Meanwhile, heat 2 tablespoons of the oil in a large frying pan over a high heat. Add the okra and a good pinch of salt. Shake the pan and leave for 1–2 minutes to crisp up on one side and then stir-fry for 2–3 minutes until completely golden. Tip the okra into the stew once the lamb is cooked. Increase the heat to medium-high and bubble away for 6–8 minutes, stirring occasionally, to reduce the sauce by half. Turn off the heat, cover and rest for 5 minutes.

4. Meanwhile, bash the remaining garlic with a little salt. Add the walnuts and remaining chopped coriander and bash until fine. Add the remaining olive oil and pomegranate molasses along with 2 tablespoons of water. Mix into a gorgeous salsa. Serve with the yakhni and Buttery Noodle Rice.

FISHERMAN'S SEAFOOD STEW

The classic seafood dish of Lebanon has to be *samke harra* (page 102), spicy fish in a tahini sauce. But it does have a little cousin, made with a tomato and pepper sauce and enriched with a drizzle of lush tahini at the end. The fish for this red *samke harra* is a whole sea bass. Sometimes I can't help but mash things up, and so delicious is the red sauce that I love packing it with a punchy mix of shellfish and chunks of sea bass, turning it into a full-blown seafood stew that screams Lebanese coastal cuisine: fresh, vibrant and packed with flavour.

SERVES 4

2 tablespoons olive oil
1 onion, finely sliced
1 large red pepper,
    finely chopped
4 garlic cloves, finely sliced
½ red chilli, finely chopped
a handful of finely chopped
    coriander leaves and stalks,
    plus extra to garnish
1 teaspoon allspice
½ teaspoon Aleppo pepper flakes
2 large tomatoes, finely chopped
2 tablespoons tomato purée
juice of 1 lemon
2 farmed sea bass fillets
    (about 100g each),
    cut into 5cm strips
300g mussels in their shells,
    picked and cleaned
4 raw giant king prawns,
    unshelled
300g squid tubes,
    cut into 2cm rings
50g tahini
15g toasted pine nuts,
    to garnish
sea salt

1. Heat the olive oil in a pan over a medium heat. Chuck in the onion and pepper and cook, stirring occasionally, for 12–15 minutes until golden. Add a splash of water after about 6–8 minutes to help soften the peppers. Add the garlic, chilli and finely chopped coriander and stir-fry for a minute. Add the allspice, Aleppo pepper flakes and a good pinch of salt. Tip in the tomatoes and tomato purée and mix everything together. Cook, stirring occasionally, for 12–14 minutes until thick.

2. Squeeze the lemon into the pan and pour in 50ml of just-boiled water. Mix well. Add the fish and seafood, cover and cook for 6–8 minutes until all the mussels have opened (discard any that have not), the prawns have turned pink and the squid and fish have cooked through. Give the pan a shake every couple of minutes to help cook evenly. Add 30g of the tahini and stir together gently.

3. Tip into a serving dish. Garnish with the pine nuts and coriander leaves and drizzle over the remaining tahini. Serve immediately.

HEARTY MOUNTAIN EGGS

[LABAN BIL BAYD]

Cooking eggs in rich garlicky yogurt might sound odd, but actually it's very common around the Eastern Mediterranean. In the cedar tree covered mountains of Lebanon, *laban bil bayd* is a hearty dish that's prepared in the spring when the yogurt has the freshest flavour. It's utterly delicious. The eggs slowly poach in the tangy yogurt, and a little garlic and dried mint pep it up with extra flavour. It's served for breakfast or a simple mid-week dinner, with loads of bread to mop up the sauce.

SERVES 2

320g full-fat Greek yogurt
1 garlic clove, crushed
¾ teaspoon dried mint
4 eggs
sea salt

1. Tip the yogurt into a shallow pan. Add the garlic, mint and a good pinch of salt. Mix well and warm through over a low heat, stirring occasionally, for 6–7 minutes.

2. Make little wells in the sauce and crack the eggs into them. Season with salt. Cook on low for 8–10 minutes until set. To help the whites cook evenly, let them firm up for a few minutes and then muddle them into the yogurt with the handle of a teaspoon. Serve immediately.

SOUK EL TAYEB VEGETABLE STEW

Eight years ago I worked in the kitchens of the Souk el Tayeb's restaurant Tawlet, one of the best restaurants in Beirut. In a very short time I learnt so much about Lebanese food. The owner, Kamal Mouzawak, is now a great friend and has been instrumental in helping me write this book. I spent a month driving around the country and meeting the most incredible local people in their homes as part of my research. But I couldn't resist going back to where it all started and doing service in the kitchen again. They had a new head chef who taught me how to make this incredible vegetable stew. I love to eat this with a fresh green salad and really crusty bread to mop up all the fabulous sauce.

SERVES 4

200g new potatoes, halved
5 tablespoons olive oil
1 aubergine, cut into 5cm chunks
2 courgettes, sliced into
   5cm pieces
2 onions, finely sliced
4 garlic cloves, roughly chopped
4 tomatoes, roughly chopped
2 tablespoons tomato purée
1 teaspoon Lebanese 7 spice
   or baharat
1 teaspoon paprika
½ teaspoon allspice
½ teaspoon ground cumin
½ teaspoon ground cinnamon
2 teaspoons dried mint
juice of ½ lemon
a handful of finely chopped
   coriander leaves
sea salt and freshly ground
   black pepper

1. Preheat the oven to 220°C/200°C fan/gas mark 7. Put the potatoes into a mixing bowl and add 1 tablespoon of the olive oil. Season with salt and pepper and toss together. Tip into a roasting dish and roast for 20 minutes until they are starting to soften at the edges.

2. Add the aubergine and courgettes to the same mixing bowl used for the potatoes and pour over 2 tablespoons of the oil. Season with salt and pepper and toss together. Tip everything into the roasting dish with the softened potatoes, shake together and roast for 20–25 minutes until everything is golden and tender.

3. Meanwhile, heat the remaining oil in a casserole over a medium heat. Add the onions and cook, stirring occasionally, for 12–15 minutes until beautifully golden. Add the garlic and mix well. Tip in the tomatoes and add the tomato purée, all the spices and dried mint. Season well with salt and pepper and pour in 200ml of just-boiled water. Mix everything together really well. Cover, reduce the heat to low and cook for 12–15 minutes or until the tomatoes have broken down into a sauce.

4. Carefully transfer the roasted vegetables to the casserole. Gently mix them into the sauce, taking care not to break them up. Add a splash of hot water if it looks too dry. Cover and cook for 5–10 minutes to allow all the flavours to marry together beautifully. The vegetables should be warmed through and the sauce really thick.

5. Squeeze the lemon into the pan and add the coriander. Give everything a final mix and serve immediately.

GREEN BEANS IN TOMATO SAUCE

Whenever I write a new book, it's home cooking that interests me the most. Generations of cooks hand down those simple dishes that they have eaten and prepared since childhood. This is one of them: an amazing everyday home-cooked meal that you'll find on dining tables across Lebanon; gorgeous green beans stewed in a lightly spiced tomato sauce. You can eat this hot or cold, with rice or solo as a simple side dish.

SERVES 4 AS A SIDE

4 tablespoons olive oil
1 onion, thinly sliced
3 garlic cloves, roughly chopped
360g runner beans, topped
   and tailed, some halved
6 tomatoes, finely chopped
2 tablespoons tomato purée
½ teaspoon allspice
¼ teaspoon ground cinnamon
sea salt

1. Heat the olive oil in a shallow pan over a medium heat. Add the onion and cook, stirring occasionally, for 8–10 minutes until golden. Add the garlic, mix well and cook for 10 seconds until fragrant.

2. Tip the beans and tomatoes into the pan. Add the tomato purée, allspice, cinnamon and a good pinch of salt. Pour over 300ml of just-boiled water and mix well. Cover, reduce the heat to low and cook for 35–40 minutes until the beans are beautifully soft.

3. Remove the lid from the pan and increase the heat to medium. Cook, stirring occasionally, for 10–15 minutes until the sauce is lovely and thick. Remove from the heat and set aside to come to room temperature. Check the salt, adding more to taste. Serve immediately.

RICE & GRAINS

DRUZE SAFFRON MANSAF

Mansaf is a typically Middle Eastern dish of lamb simmered in yogurt. This is a wonderful Druze version that my friend Rima cooked for lunch in Ramliyeh, a little village in the Chouf Mountains. Surrounded by friends, we feasted in her tiny living room. After we ate, she brought out the typically Druze drink *yerba mate*, a highly caffeinated brew from Argentina introduced to the Levant by Syrians in the nineteenth century. The ladies drank it from a round wooden mug called a *karaa* using a metal straw or *bombilla*. I took a huge lug and – much to the amusement of my hosts – gagged on the acrid taste. I'll stick to Rima's *mansaf* any day.

SERVES 4

4 lamb shanks
3 tablespoons olive oil
2 litres hot lamb stock
1 cinnamon stick (about 10cm)
2.5cm piece of ginger,
   sliced thinly
3 bay leaves
20g butter
1 onion, finely chopped
1 teaspoon Lebanese 7 spice
   or baharat
¼ teaspoon ground cinnamon
250g bulgur
pinch of saffron strands
1 teaspoon cornflour
300g Labna (see page 24)
sea salt and freshly ground
   black pepper

To *garnish*
a handful of roughly chopped
   mint leaves
15g toasted pine nuts
15g toasted flaked almonds

1. Season the lamb with salt and pepper. Heat 2 tablespoons of the olive oil in a large casserole over a medium–high heat and brown the lamb for 4–5 minutes on two sides. Pour over the stock. It should cover the lamb by about three quarters. Add the cinnamon, ginger and bay leaves. Bring to the boil, cover, reduce the heat to low and cook for 2–2½ hours or until the lamb is beautifully tender. Leaving the lamb in the stock to rest, measure off 550ml of the stock to use in the bulgur.

2. Melt the butter with the remaining oil in a saucepan over a medium heat. Add the onion and cook, stirring occasionally, for 6–8 minutes until golden. Add the Lebanese 7 spice, cinnamon and a good pinch of salt. Mix well. Add the bulgur and mix together. Pour in the reserved lamb stock and bring to the boil. Cover, reduce the heat to low and cook for 30–35 minutes until tender. Remove from the heat and fluff up the bulgur with a fork.

3. Take the lamb shanks out of the stock and place on a warm serving dish. Cover and set aside. Strain the stock and pour 450ml back into the casserole. Bring to the boil over a medium heat. Add a pinch of salt and the saffron, and whisk together.

4. Put the cornflour in a bowl with 2 tablespoons of water. Mix together and tip into the casserole with the boiling stock. Whisk together to thicken.

5. Reduce the heat to low and tip the labna into the pan. Whisk again until you have a lovely smooth sauce. Return the lamb shanks to the casserole, cover and leave to stand for 5 minutes so that the hot sauce warms through the lamb.

6. Transfer the lamb shanks to the serving dish and pour over the sauce. Garnish with the mint leaves, pine nuts and almonds. Serve immediately with the bulgur.

MAKLOUBEH

Makloubeh, meaning 'up-side-down cake', is a delicious rice dish found all over the Middle East. Vegetables are layered into the bottom of a pot and then meat and rice are cooked on top. When ready, you cover the pot with a plate and flip the glorious *makloubeh* out. This is my lovely Lebanese version that I picked up in Beirut. The trick is to use a shallow non-stick saucepan so that when you flip the dish over, the ingredients don't have far to fall and hold their shape. I love to shower my *makloubeh* with toasted nuts and herbs to add to the overall decadence of the dish. They also cover a multitude of sins just in case it breaks. Well, we can't be perfect every time.

SERVES 6

1 aubergine, sliced
   into 1cm rounds
300g cauliflower florets
500g skinless, boneless
   chicken thigh fillets
6 tablespoons olive oil
3½ teaspoons allspice
1 onion, finely chopped
400g Basmati rice
1½ teaspoons Lebanese 7 spice
   or baharat
1 teaspoon paprika
700ml hot chicken stock
2 tablespoons tomato purée
40g toasted cashew nuts
40g toasted almonds
15g toasted pine nuts
a handful of finely chopped
   parsley leaves
sea salt

For the yogurt sauce
200g full-fat Greek yogurt
½ garlic clove, mashed
juice of ¼ lemon
sea salt

1. Preheat the oven to 220°C/200°C fan/gas mark 7. Put the aubergine, cauliflower, chicken, 3 tablespoons of the olive oil, 2 teaspoons of the allspice and a good pinch of salt into a mixing bowl and mix everything together. Tip into a baking dish and roast for 30–35 minutes until everything is cooked through and tender.

2. Heat 2 tablespoons of the olive oil in a shallow, non-stick saucepan over a medium heat. Add the onion and cook, stirring occasionally, for 6–8 minutes until golden. Add the rice to the pan along with the Lebanese 7 spice, paprika, the remaining allspice and a really good pinch of salt. Mix well, then tip into a bowl.

3. Brush the remaining oil over the base of the same pan used to cook the onion. Layer the aubergine across the bottom of the pan and then add the cauliflower. Shred the chicken over the top and tip the rice over everything. Even it out with the back of a spoon.

4. Mix the stock and tomato purée together in a jug and pour over the rice. Bring to the boil over a medium heat, cover, reduce the heat to low and cook for 20 minutes until the rice has absorbed all the liquid. Turn off the heat and leave to stand, covered, for 10 minutes. This will fluff the rice up beautifully.

5. Meanwhile, make the yogurt sauce. Mix the yogurt with the garlic, lemon and a good pinch of salt in a serving bowl.

6. Remove the lid from the rice and place a large serving dish over the top of the pan. In one quick movement, flip the pan onto the plate. Tap the side of the pan and leave for 10 seconds and then slowly lift the pan up from the plate. The makloubeh should fall out in one piece. No worries if anything breaks up, just scoop it out of the pan and make good. Scatter over the toasted nuts and parsley – they can hide anything – and serve immediately with the yogurt sauce.

ABU'S SPICED LAMB FREEKEH

Just outside the dusty town of Nabatieh in the far south of Lebanon, Abu Kassam has made a living from growing the wonderfully fragrant herb za'atar. People thought he was mad to commercialise something that grew wild. Well, he did it, and now he supplies businesses all over the world with this incredible ingredient. The area is home to a poor rural community and Abu, who has done well for himself, began buying freekeh from the local women to package and sell. He gives them an inflated price on the promise of getting the best grains. The taste and texture are fabulous and work so well in this simple dish of spiced lamb and freekeh, a classic combination that is so typical of southern Lebanese cooking.

SERVES 6

For the lamb
6 garlic cloves, peeled
250g full-fat Greek yogurt
zest and juice of 1 lemon
2 teaspoons Lebanese 7 spice
   or baharat
1 teaspoon allspice
½ teaspoon cinnamon
2 teaspoons dried mint
1.5kg butterflied leg of lamb
3 tablespoons olive oil
sea salt

For the freekeh
20g butter
200g minced lamb with
   15–20 per cent fat
1 teaspoon Lebanese 7 spice
   or baharat
1 teaspoon allspice
300g freekeh
700ml hot lamb stock
sea salt

For the garnish
20g toasted cashew nuts
20g toasted almonds
a small handful of finely
   chopped parsley leaves

1. Mash the garlic into a paste with a little salt and tip into a mixing bowl. Add the yogurt, lemon zest and juice, spices and dried mint. Season with a really good pinch of salt and mix well. Slather this gorgeous marinade all over the lamb and leave in the fridge to work its magic overnight.

2. Preheat the oven to 220°C/200°C fan/gas mark 7 and take the lamb out of the fridge to come to room temperature. Place the lamb on a grilling rack over a roasting dish and brush the top with the olive oil. Roast for 30–35 minutes until charred on the outside and still pink in the middle. Remove from the oven and transfer the lamb to a warm dish. Cover with foil and leave to rest for 10 minutes. Pour the juices from the roasting tray into a jug.

3. Meanwhile, make the freekeh. Melt the butter in a frying pan over a high heat and add the minced lamb. Stir-fry for 3–4 minutes until just cooked through. Add the spices and a good pinch of salt. Mix well, then add the freekeh to the pan and pour over the stock. Stir together and bring to the boil. Cover, reduce the heat to low and cook for 40–45 minutes or until all the liquid has gone and the freekeh is lovely and tender. Remove from the heat and leave to rest for 5 minutes.

4. To serve, tip the freekeh onto a serving dish. Slice up the lamb and lay it over the top. Pour over the reserved lamb juices, scatter with the nuts and parsley and serve immediately.

SLEEPY HARBOUR HAKE

Sayadieh-bi-samak – fish with rice and onions – is a lovely local dish from the seaside town of Saida, or Sidon. This is a simple supper; a mid-week meal that your mum would make for you after a long day. The fish is rubbed in garlic and then cooked with rice, caramelised onions and loads of mellow spices. All the flavours come together beautifully in the pan and it's all finished off with a velvety tarator sauce. You can use any white fish to make this recipe but I have gone for hake – its meaty fillets can really stand up to the spices.

SERVES 4

6 garlic cloves, crushed
1½ teaspoons allspice
1½ teaspoons ground cumin
6 tablespoons olive oil
4 hake fillets (about 150g each)
2 onions, finely chopped
1 teaspoon Lebanese 7 spice
 or baharat
1 cinnamon stick (about 10cm)
4 cardamom pods, bashed
300g Basmati rice
600ml hot chicken or fish stock
a small handful of finely
 chopped mint leaves
a small handful of finely
 chopped coriander leaves
20g toasted flaked almonds,
 to garnish
sea salt

For the tarator sauce
80g tahini
juice of ½ lemon
sea salt

1. Mash four of the garlic cloves with a good pinch of salt. Add ½ teaspoon allspice, 1 teaspoon cumin and 2 tablespoons of the olive oil. Mix well into a paste. Put the fish into a mixing bowl and add the spice paste. Mix well so the hake is completely covered.

2. Heat 2 tablespoons of the oil in a large pan over a medium heat. Place the fish, skin side down, into the pan and fry for 2–3 minutes until lovely and golden. Remove from the pan and set aside.

3. Pour the remaining oil into the pan and add the onions. Cook, stirring occasionally, for 10–12 minutes until golden. Stir in the remaining garlic, allspice and cumin, and add the Lebanese 7 spice, cinnamon stick and cardamom. Tip the rice into the pan, mix well and pour over the stock.

4. Put the fish into the pan and nestle the fillets into the rice and stock. Bring to the boil, cover, reduce the heat to low and cook for 12–15 minutes until the rice is tender and the fish cooked through. Remove from the heat and leave to stand for 5 minutes. Remove the fish and set aside. Season the rice with a good pinch of salt and add most of the herbs. Fluff up with a fork and tip onto a serving dish. Top with the fish and garnish with the remaining herbs and toasted almonds.

5. Meanwhile, make the tarator sauce. Mix the tahini, lemon juice and a good pinch of salt with 65ml of water into a creamy sauce. Serve immediately with the fish and rice.

BEQAA VALLEY SALAD

[WARAK ENAB]

Set on the lower slopes of the mountains overlooking the vineyards of the Beqaa Valley is the gorgeous little village of Ammiq. The local women make a fantastic vegetarian dish of stuffed vine leaves or *warak enab*. I loved the filling and before it was even cooked I was all over it, eating spoonfuls straight from the mixing bowl: soft rice with a few tomatoes, onions and herbs and a generous glug of pomegranate molasses. I have bulked out the recipe to make a sensational side salad that's good with any barbecued meats, grilled fish or roasted vegetables.

SERVES 4–6 AS A SIDE

200g Basmati rice
200g cherry tomatoes, halved
½ red onion, finely chopped
a large handful of finely chopped
   parsley leaves
a handful of roughly chopped
   oregano leaves
juice of 1 lemon
3 tablespoons pomegranate
   molasses
2 tablespoons olive oil
1 teaspoon sumac
sea salt

1. Cook the rice for 10–12 minutes in a large pan of boiling water until tender. Drain and refresh under cold running water, then drain again thoroughly.

2. Tip the rice into a mixing bowl and add the tomatoes, onion, parsley, oregano, lemon juice, pomegranate molasses, olive oil, sumac and a really good pinch of salt. Mix everything together really well so that the lovely flavours of the lemon and pomegranate molasses coat the rice. Tip into a serving bowl and tuck in.

SPRING BROAD BEAN & CORIANDER PILAF

Fava beans or *ful*, which we call broad beans, are very popular in Lebanon. Throughout the year the dried beans are used to make hummus *ful*, made with cooked fava beans, chickpeas, lemon and tahini, which is a popular breakfast dish. In spring, when the *ful* are plentiful, they are used generously in various meze dishes, crisp salads and this wonderful pilaf. The beans are cooked with lots of garlic and cumin to accentuate their fresh flavour.

SERVES 4

2 tablespoons olive oil
1 onion, finely chopped
3 garlic cloves, finely chopped
1 teaspoon cumin seeds
a handful of finely chopped
    coriander leaves and stalks,
    separated
100g fresh or frozen podded
    broad beans
200g long-grain rice
500ml hot vegetable stock
sea salt

1. Heat the olive oil in a saucepan over a medium heat. Add the onion and a good pinch of salt. Cook, stirring occasionally, for 5–6 minutes until soft.

2. Add the garlic, cumin, coriander stalks and half the leaves to the pan. Add a little pinch of salt and mix well. Stir-fry for about 30 seconds until fragrant and then tip the broad beans and rice into the pan. Gently mix together to coat the rice in the oil and then pour over the stock. Bring to the boil, cover, reduce the heat to low and cook for 12–15 minutes until all the liquid has been absorbed.

3. Remove the pan from the heat, cover and rest for 10 minutes so that the rice can fluff up. Scatter the remaining coriander into the pan and mix together using a fork. Serve immediately.

FIG, WALNUT & FREEKEH SALAD

Freekeh is a wonderful ancient grain that's low in fat and high in protein, fibre, calcium and zinc. The name comes from the Arabic word *farak*, meaning 'to rub', in reference to how the farmers extract the grain by rubbing the wheat between their hands. Grown in the south of Lebanon, wheat is harvested when it's still young and green in colour. Great mounds of wheat are then roasted over a fire, giving the freekeh its distinctive smoky flavour. It can really take robust flavours and is wonderful in a pilaf or hearty salad.

**SERVES 2 AS A MAIN
OR 4 AS A SIDE**

160g freekeh
4 spring onions, finely chopped
a small handful of finely
   chopped coriander leaves
2 small handfuls of finely
   chopped mint leaves
2 tablespoons olive oil,
   plus extra for drizzling
3 tablespoons pomegranate
   molasses
50g walnuts, bashed
   into a fine rubble
1½ teaspoons sumac
4 figs, quartered
50g feta
sea salt

1. Tip the freekeh into a pan and pour over plenty of just-boiled water. Bring to the boil over a high heat. Cover, reduce the heat to low and simmer for 20–25 minutes until tender but still with a good bite. Drain, refresh under cold running water, then drain again thoroughly.

2. Put the freekeh into a large mixing bowl and add the spring onions, coriander, half the mint, 1 tablespoon of the olive oil, 2 tablespoons of the pomegranate molasses, 30g of the walnuts, 1 teaspoon of the sumac and a really good pinch of salt. Mix everything together really well and tip into a salad bowl.

3. Arrange the figs on top of the freekeh and crumble over the feta. Scatter with the remaining walnuts, sumac and mint. Drizzle the remaining olive oil and pomegranate molasses over the top and serve immediately.

RICE WITH LENTILS
[MUJADDARA]

This wonderfully warming, cheap and cheerful rice recipe is a staple dish found on tables all over Lebanon. The rice is cooked with lentils and spices, and served with masses of caramelised onions. It's a meal in itself, the lentils adding protein, but *mujaddara* also makes a fabulous side dish.

SERVES 4

4 tablespoons olive oil
3 onions, 1 finely chopped
    and 2 finely sliced
2 garlic cloves, finely chopped
150g brown lentils, washed
550ml vegetable stock
    (made with ½ stock cube)
150g long grain rice
1 teaspoon ground cumin
½ teaspoon Lebanese 7 spice
    or baharat
sea salt

1. Heat 2 tablespoons of the olive oil in a saucepan over a medium heat. Add the finely chopped onion and cook, stirring occasionally, for 6–8 minutes until just golden. Add the garlic and stir-fry for 30 seconds until fragrant.

2. Tip the lentils into the pan with the onion and pour over the stock. Bring to the boil, cover, reduce the heat to low and cook for 20 minutes to soften the lentils. Add the rice, cumin, Lebanese 7 spice and a good pinch of salt. Mix well, cover and cook for a further 20 minutes or until all the water has been absorbed and the rice and lentils are tender. Add a little extra water if the lentils need more cooking. Remove from the heat, cover and rest for 10 minutes. Stir with a fork to separate the rice grains and lentils.

3. Meanwhile, heat the remaining oil in a non-stick frying pan over a low–medium heat. Add the sliced onions and a good pinch of salt. Mix well and cook, stirring occasionally, for 25–30 minutes or until the onions have completely caramelised and are gorgeously golden and crispy.

4. Tip the mujaddara onto a serving dish and top with the onions. Serve immediately.

BUTTERY NOODLE RICE

This is another rustic rice recipe, made with smashed vermicelli noodles browned in butter and then cooked with rice until tender, giving the dish a wonderful two-toned texture. It's a staple side to stews and kebabs, but you know what? I love it in a bowl with nothing else but a spoon to dig in: killer comfort food.

SERVES 4–6 AS A SIDE

50g butter
55g vermicelli egg noodles,
    broken into small pieces
300g long grain rice
sea salt

1. Melt the butter in a large pan over a medium heat. Add the noodles and stir-fry for 3–4 minutes until golden. Add the rice to the pan and mix together in the butter. Pour over 600ml just-boiled water, cover, reduce the heat to low and cook for 10–12 minutes until the water has been absorbed. Remove from the heat, cover and leave to stand for 10 minutes.

2. Season the rice with a pinch of salt and mix together with a fork. Tip onto a warm serving dish and serve immediately.

CUMIN & CARAWAY SPICED LEBANESE COUSCOUS
[MOGHRABIEH]

Moghrabieh is a celebratory dish meaning 'from the Maghreb', which is thought to be the origin of this recipe. *Moghrabieh* is both the name of the finished dish and the pearls of rolled durum wheat semolina (also known as Lebanese couscous) used to make it. Like pasta, the rolled dough needs to be cooked out, and then it's added to a wonderful chicken broth flavoured with caraway and cumin. Unlike pasta, Lebanese couscous has a much firmer texture. This is Arabic food at its best: richly spiced, deeply savoury and incredibly filling. In the souks of Tripoli, *moghrabieh* is a street food. At El Dabousi, a little shop started by his grandfather over 100 years ago, Mohammed serves this in flatbread with tangy pickles. It's a rather wonderful way to cut through the richness of the dish.

SERVES 4–6

2 tablespoons olive oil
1kg chicken thighs, skin on and bone in
6 baby shallots, peeled
8 garlic cloves, peeled
2 teaspoons ground caraway, plus a pinch for serving
2 teaspoons ground cumin
2 teaspoons Lebanese 7 spice or baharat
1 cinnamon stick (about 10cm)
500ml hot chicken stock
350g moghrabieh (Lebanese couscous)
20g butter
140g drained chickpeas
zest of 1 lemon and juice of ½ lemon
a small handful of coriander leaves, to garnish
sea salt

1. Heat the olive oil in a large casserole over a medium heat. Put the chicken into the pan skin side down and add the shallots. Cook for 8–10 minutes, browning the chicken skin and turning the shallots every few minutes until golden. Turn the chicken and add the garlic. Cook for 2 minutes to get some colour on the garlic. Add the caraway, cumin, Lebanese 7 spice and cinnamon. Pour over the stock and bring to the boil. Cover, reduce the heat to low and cook for 40–45 minutes until the chicken is cooked through and tender.

2. Meanwhile, parboil the moghrabieh for 15 minutes in a pan of boiling water and then drain. Return to the pan and add the butter. Mix well and tip into the pan with the cooked chicken. Add the chickpeas and shake the pan so that the moghrabieh settles into the sauce. Cover and cook for 15 minutes until tender. Remove the lid and increase the heat a little. Cook, shaking the pan occasionally, for 10–12 minutes until the sauce is lovely and thick, and clinging like old friends to the moghrabieh. Squeeze the lemon juice into the pan and mix well. Check the seasoning and add salt to taste.

3. To serve, tip the moghrabieh into a serving dish and arrange the chicken over the top. Garnish with the lemon zest, coriander and a pinch of caraway. Serve immediately.

BREADS & PASTRIES

SUMAC-SPICED LAMB PITTAS

[ARAYES KAFTA]

In El Mina, the old Phoenician part of Tripoli, Ammaah has run his family bakery for more than fifty years and makes the best pittas in town: fluffy, soft and utterly dreamy. The dark, charred wooden walls tell the story of more than five hundred breads he produces every day in the swelteringly hot oven. This part of the medina is effectively the high street and those in the know buy Ammaah's pittas and take them over the road to the butcher's shop, where they stuff the breads with a mix of well-seasoned lamb and tomatoes and roast them off in their makeshift oven until crisp. It's dude food, cooked on the spot and served with lemon wedges: the perfect snack before a morning's shopping in the souk.

MAKES 8

For the filling
½ onion, roughly chopped
1 tomato, roughly chopped
250g minced lamb with
    15–20 per cent fat
1 teaspoon sumac
½ teaspoon Lebanese 7 spice
    or baharat
½ teaspoon allspice
a small handful of parsley leaves
sea salt

8 small round pitta breads
2 tablespoons olive oil
lemon wedges, to serve

1. Preheat the oven to 220°C/200°C fan/gas mark 7. Begin with the filling. Put the onion into a food-processor and blend until fine. Add the tomato, lamb, sumac, Lebanese 7 spice, allspice, parsley and a good pinch of salt. Blend until lovely and smooth.

2. Put each pitta into the microwave for 20–30 seconds to puff up and soften. Using a serrated knife, cut around the edge of the pitta and carefully open it up, leaving a tiny section uncut to hold it together. Repeat with the rest.

3. Spread the lamb mixture over one half of the inside of each pitta. Close them up and place on a grill rack. Brush with olive oil and roast in the oven for 6–8 minutes until the lamb is cooked and really juicy. Cut into quarters and serve immediately with lemon wedges.

BAALBEK SFIHA

Baalbek, favourably situated in the fertile Beqaa Valley, is best known for two things: its fabulous Roman ruins and the highest-quality meat in Lebanon. Early one morning, I went to meet Zachariah, a local baker known for making the best *sfiha* – meat pastries – in town. There are plenty of different types of *sfiha* all over the country. Zachariah's were the classic diamond shape but he went meat-heavy with a super thin and crispy pastry – far better, in my opinion, than the dryer, doughy ones I've had in the past. Watching him prepare the pastries was spellbinding. He expertly whipped up a batch of fluffy dough, separating it out into portions and smacking each one into flat rounds in seconds. I could taste all that passion and energy in each mouthful. They make the perfect appetiser or light lunch with a crunchy green salad.

MAKES 24 LITTLE PASTRIES

For the dough
400g plain flour, plus extra
    for dusting
7g sachet fast-action yeast
2 teaspoons salt
1 teaspoon caster sugar
60ml vegetable oil,
    plus extra for oiling

For the filling
2 tomatoes, roughly chopped
400g minced lamb,
    with 20 per cent fat
1 teaspoon allspice
1 teaspoon Lebanese 7 spice
    or baharat
sea salt

lemon wedges, to serve

1. Tip the flour into a mixing bowl and add the yeast, salt and sugar. Mix well. Make a well in the centre and pour in the oil. Add 180ml water and bring together into a dough. If the mixture looks too dry, add a splash more water. Tip onto a floured surface and knead for 6–7 minutes until smooth. Pop into an oiled mixing bowl, cover and leave to rest for 10 minutes.

2. Tip the dough onto a floured surface and divide into 24 portions. Use your hands to shape into balls and dust each one with a little flour. Roll each one into a 10cm round with a rolling pin: they are rough and ready so don't worry about being too perfect.

3. Meanwhile, put the tomatoes into a food-processor and blend until fine. Tip into a mixing bowl and add the lamb, allspice, Lebanese 7 spice and a good pinch of salt. Mix together really well.

4. Preheat the oven to 220°C/200°C fan/gas mark 7 and line a few baking trays with oiled baking paper. Put 1 tablespoon (25g) of meat in the centre of one of the rounds of dough. Even it out a little but not quite to the edge. Now pinch in four points of the circle to make a square. Start by pinching two opposite sides of the circle inwards to make an oval shape. Do the same with the two remaining curved sides to form a square. You want to be quite firm so that you pull the circular edges of the pastry inwards and just over the meat filling. Gently press the whole thing down to flatten and pop onto one of the baking sheets. Repeat with the remaining circles. Bake for 15–20 minutes until golden. Remove from the oven and season with a little salt. Leave to cool slightly, before serving with lemon wedges.

ZA'ATAR MAN'OUCHE

Man'ouche is a breakfast bread, one of the national dishes of Lebanon, and is cooked in little bakeries all over the country. It is thin, crisp and charred and primarily served with za'atar-infused oil liberally brushed all over it. The breads are often stuffed with herbs and rolled up so you can tuck into them while walking to work. It's also totally socially acceptable to have a *man'ouche* covered in cheese first thing in the morning. I love mine with both cheese and za'atar, and stuffed with fresh mint. Oh, and an Arabic coffee on the side is a must. Traditionally *man'ouche* is cooked in a wood-fired oven, which is what gives the bread the right crispiness and smoky flavour. I think the best way to replicate this at home is in a very hot, non-stick frying pan. It gives the smack of heat that you need. Just watch the temperature and if the bread looks as if it's getting a little burnt on the bottom, turn down the heat so it can cook through evenly.

MAKES 8

For the dough
400g plain flour,
     plus extra for dusting
7g sachet fast-action yeast
2 teaspoons salt
1 teaspoon sugar
2 tablespoons olive oil,
     plus extra for oiling

For the topping
8 tablespoons olive oil
4 tablespoons za'atar
80g feta, crumbled
a large handful of mint leaves
sea salt

1. Tip the flour into a mixing bowl and add the yeast, salt and sugar. Mix well. Make a well in the centre and pour in the oil. Add 250ml water and bring together into a dough. If the mixture looks too dry, add a splash more water, up to an additional 30ml. Tip onto a floured surface and knead for 6–7 minutes until smooth. Pop into an oiled mixing bowl, cover and leave to rest for 1 hour in a cool, dark spot in the kitchen.

2. Divide the dough into eight portions. Take one portion and flatten into a round. Sprinkle both sides with a little flour and roll out thinly into a 20cm diameter circle. Repeat with the remaining dough.

3. For the topping, mix the olive oil with the za'atar and a good pinch of salt in a bowl.

4. Heat a non-stick frying pan over a medium–high heat and add one of the circles of dough. Generously brush the top with the za'atar oil. Turn down the heat to medium–low and cook for about 2–2½ minutes until the bottom is beautifully charred and the top of the dough cooked. You have to watch carefully, adjusting the heat so that the bread isn't cooking too quickly or too slowly. Remove from the pan and repeat with the remaining circles. Garnish with a little feta and a few mint leaves. Serve immediately.

MOUNTAIN BREAKFAST BREAD

Before a particularly challenging hike up onto the cliffs of Qadisha Valley, I met my guide, George, for breakfast at the Hard Bakery in the tiny village of Hadath el Jebbeh overlooking the lush Qannoubine Valley. It was obviously the place to be, packed with locals and a few rowdy young military men, all tucking into huge pastries stuffed with lamb and kishk – dried fermented yogurt with an intense creamy flavour. The pastry was divine and the perfect fuel-up before walking. Rather than making kishk, I just mix cooked meat with good quality labna. It tastes just as good.

MAKES 4

For the dough
200g plain flour, plus extra for dusting
3.5g (½ sachet) fast-action yeast
1 teaspoon salt
½ teaspoon sugar
1 tablespoon olive oil, plus extra for oiling

For the filling
4 tablespoons olive oil
1 onion, finely chopped
250g lamb mince with 15–20 per cent fat
2 garlic cloves, crushed
1 teaspoon allspice
230g Labna (see page 24)
sea salt and freshly ground black pepper

1. Tip the flour into a mixing bowl and add the yeast, salt and sugar. Mix well. Make a well in the centre and pour in the oil. Add 100ml water and bring together into a dough. If the mixture looks too dry, add a splash more water, up to an extra 25ml. Tip onto a floured surface and knead for 6–7 minutes until smooth. Pop into an oiled mixing bowl, cover and leave to rest for 1 hour in a cool, dark spot in the kitchen.

2. Meanwhile, make the filling. Heat 2 tablespoons of the olive oil in a frying pan over a high heat. Add the onion, lamb, garlic and a good pinch of salt and pepper. Stir-fry for 8–10 minutes until cooked through and golden. Turn off the heat and add the allspice. Mix well and tip into a bowl. Leave to cool completely. Add the labna and mix together. Check the seasoning and add salt to taste.

3. Preheat the oven to 220°C/200°C fan/gas mark 7 and line a baking sheet with oiled baking paper. Divide into four portions and form each one into a ball. Dust them with flour and roll out thinly into 15cm diameter rounds.

4. Put a quarter of the filling into the centre of one of the rounds of dough. Wet your finger and run it around the edge of the circle to help it seal. Pull three points of the circle into the centre to create a triangle shape. Crimp the edges together so that they are sealed tightly. Pop this onto a baking sheet and repeat with the remaining circles.

5. Brush the tops of the breads with the remaining olive oil and season with a good pinch of salt. Bake for 18–20 minutes until lightly golden. Remove from the oven and leave to cool for 5 minutes before serving.

GEORGINA'S SPINACH FATTAYAH

Driving in Lebanon has its highs and lows. It's wonderful to be able to go where you want and take in the stunning scenery. But there are challenges. Road signs, if any, are in Arabic, which I can't read, and street names are non-existent. After a particularly hair-raising drive from Tripoli to a little mountain village to meet my friend Georgina, I rolled up, slightly dishevelled, and promptly crashed into her garage. She spotted the desperation in my eyes and calmly fed me her famous spinach *fattayah*. They proved to be the ultimate tonic after my journey, and bonus, she gave me her recipe.

MAKES 8

For the dough
150 plain flour, plus extra
  for dusting
50g wholemeal flour
3.5g (½ sachet) fast-action yeast
1 teaspoon salt
½ teaspoon sugar
2 tablespoons olive oil,
  plus extra for oiling

For the filling
200g spinach
2 tomatoes
1 onion, finely chopped
juice of 1 lemon
2 teaspoons sumac
1 teaspoon allspice
1 tablespoon olive oil
50ml whole milk
sea salt and freshly ground
  black pepper

1. Put the two flours into a mixing bowl and add the yeast, salt and sugar. Mix together. Make a well in the centre and pour in the oil. Add 100ml water and bring together into a dough. If the mixture looks too dry, add a splash more water, up to an additional 25ml. Tip onto a floured surface and knead for 6–7 minutes until smooth. Pop into an oiled mixing bowl, cover and leave to rest for 1 hour in a cool, dark spot in the kitchen.

2. Divide into eight portions. Form each one into a ball, dust them with flour, then roll them out into 10–12cm rounds.

3. To make the filling, put the spinach into a mixing bowl and squeeze it really hard between your hands – scrunching it up like this makes it easier to work with. Tip onto a chopping board and finely chop. Return to the bowl. Cut the tomatoes in half and squeeze out the pips. You don't want them as they will make the filling too watery. Finely chop the flesh and add to the spinach. Add the onion, lemon, sumac, allspice, olive oil and a good pinch of salt and pepper. Mix together really well.

4. Preheat the oven to 180°C fan/200°C/gas mark 6 and line a baking sheet with oiled baking paper. Wet your finger and run it around the edge of each circle to help it seal. Top each round of dough with an equal amount of the filling. Pull three points of a circle into the centre to create a triangle shape. Crimp the edges together so that they seal tightly. Pop this onto a baking sheet and repeat with the remaining circles. Brush the tops with a little milk and bake for 12–15 minutes until just golden on top. Leave to cool completely and then serve.

POMEGRANATE & TAHINI BEEF PASTRIES
[LAHM BAJINE]

Made with very thin pastry, almost like puff pastry, then stuffed with a creamy mix of tahini, pomegranate molasses and spices, these perfect party snacks are fabulous to serve as canapés.

MAKES 20 PASTRIES

For the dough
200g plain flour, plus
    extra for dusting
3.5g (½ sachet) fast-action yeast
1 teaspoon salt
1 teaspoon sugar
1 tablespoon olive oil
50g butter, melted

For the filling
1½ tablespoons olive oil
15g toasted pine nuts
½ onion, finely chopped
170g beef mince with
    15–20 per cent fat
¾ teaspoon allspice
1 tablespoon red wine vinegar
1 teaspoon dried mint
200g Greek yogurt
1 tablespoon tahini
2 tablespoons pomegranate
    molasses
sea salt

For the dipping sauce
200g Greek yogurt
½ garlic clove, mashed
juice of ½ lemon
1 teaspoon dried mint
sea salt

1. To make the dough, mix the flour, yeast, salt and sugar in a bowl. Pour in the oil and 125ml water. Bring together into a dough and tip onto a floured surface. Knead for 5–6 minutes until pale and smooth, then halve.

2. Brush a clean work surface with some of the melted butter. Take a portion of dough and flatten it into a circle. Rub a little butter on your hands and rub them over both sides of the dough. Using your fingers, work the dough into a wide circle about 45cm in diameter. Don't worry if the dough tears a little; just try to get it as thin as possible. Very loosely roll up the dough into a cigar shape and place on a greased plate. Repeat with the other portion. Cover with clingfilm and chill for 1 hour in the fridge.

3. Meanwhile, make your filling. Heat the oil in a pan over a high heat. Add the pine nuts, onion and beef and stir-fry for 8–10 minutes until golden. Add the allspice and a good pinch of salt. Mix well and transfer to a mixing bowl. Set aside to cool completely. Pour the vinegar into the bowl, add the mint, yogurt, tahini and pomegranate molasses and mix everything together. Add more salt if needed.

4. Preheat the oven to 200°C/180°C fan/gas mark 6. Take the dough out of the fridge and cut each portion into ten pieces. Brush a clean work surface with some of the melted butter and rub a little on your hands. Flatten one of the pieces of dough into a circle about 7–10cm in diameter. It should quite thin. Place 1 teaspoon of the filling in the centre of the circle, slightly towards the bottom. Spread out into a horizontal line. Fold in the sides of the circle, just over the filling, then tightly roll up the dough away from you into a neat cigar shape. Place on a baking sheet lined with oiled baking paper. Repeat with the rest, spacing them well apart on the baking sheet. Bake for 12–15 minutes until just golden. Leave to cool for 5–10 minutes.

5. While the lahm bajine cool, mix the yogurt with the garlic, lemon juice, 2–3 tablespoons of water, the dried mint and a good pinch of salt into a smooth dipping sauce. Serve immediately with the lahm bajine, which should be slightly warmer than room temperature.

SAIDA SAUSAGE ROLLS

Calling this recipe a sausage roll feels a little like underselling it. The Arabic name for this dish is *lahm bajine*, a meat bread made in different guises everywhere all over Lebanon. I discovered this version in Saida. Down one of the city's many narrow stone alleyways in the souk, a wonderful old man had a tiny bakery, only an oven in an arch really, where he displayed these moreish snacks on rustic wooden trays. I devoured several of them, piping hot from the oven. Heavy with tart sumac and with the crispest pastry, they had such an interesting flavour. I know I would be scolded for doing so, but I find using shop-bought, ready-rolled puff pastry gives the perfect texture.

MAKES 8

2 tablespoons olive oil,
   plus extra for brushing
1 onion, finely chopped
250g beef mince with
   15–20 per cent fat
2 tablespoons sumac, plus
   a little extra for sprinkling
1 teaspoon allspice
¼ teaspoon ground cinnamon
320g pack ready-rolled
   puff pastry
flour, for dusting
sea salt

1. Heat the oil in a pan over a medium heat and add the onion and a good pinch of salt. Cook, stirring occasionally, for 6–8 minutes until golden. Tip into a mixing bowl and add the beef, 1 tablespoon of the sumac, the allspice and the cinnamon. Season with a little salt and mix well so that the spices are completely combined with the meat.

2. Preheat the oven to 200°C/180°C fan/gas mark 6. Lay the pastry on a clean, lightly floured work surface. Sprinkle the remaining sumac evenly over the pastry and gently press it in. This gives your rolls a lovely tart kick. Cut the pastry in half lengthways and then cut each long piece into four, to make eight rectangles.

3. Place a portion of the filling in a line, lengthways, down the centre of one of the rectangles of pastry. Roll up into a sausage roll and place, fold side down, on a baking sheet lined with oiled baking paper. Repeat with the rest. Brush the tops of each pastry with olive oil and then scatter a little salt and sumac over each one. Bake for 15–20 minutes until golden and risen. Remove from the oven and leave to cool for a few minutes before serving.

DRUZE BREAKFAST BREADS

My first taste of the Druze community in Lebanon was meeting my friend Rima in her lovely little village, Ramliyeh, in the lush Chouf Mountains. We strolled down the quiet backstreets to a little bakery to grab breakfast. For me, this was already a real treat, as the Druze are known for their breadmaking skills. The shop was run by a striking woman, veiled in a long white robe, the traditional dress for a highly religious Druze lady. With expert skill she worked some dough into a neat nest to make a dish called *man'ouche bida qawarma*, a flatbread with egg and preserved lamb's tail; essentially a Druze McMuffin. She spread the highly seasoned meat and some of the fat across the dough and then cracked an egg into the centre of the nest. After a few minutes in the roaring heat of the oven it came out crispy and golden. We took the bread home and enjoyed it with tea. What an introduction to this incredible community. Preserved lamb's tail – *qawarma* – won't be easy to come by, so here I use minced lamb instead.

MAKES 4

For the dough
400g plain flour, plus
   extra for dusting
7g sachet fast-action yeast
2 teaspoons salt
1 teaspoon caster sugar
2 tablespoons olive oil,
   plus extra for oiling
100ml whole milk

For the filling
140g minced lamb with
   20 per cent fat
½ teaspoon allspice,
   plus extra for seasoning
4 eggs
sea salt

1. Put the flour, yeast, salt and sugar into a bowl. Stir together and make a well in the centre. Pour in the olive oil, milk and 150ml water. Bring together into a dough. If it's too dry, add a few teaspoons of water. Tip onto a floured surface and knead for 6–7 minutes until smooth. Put the dough into an oiled mixing bowl, cover and leave to rest for 1 hour in a cool, dark spot in the kitchen.

2. Meanwhile, mix the lamb with the allspice and a good pinch of salt in a bowl.

3. Preheat the oven to 200°C/180°C fan/gas mark 6. Knock the air out of the dough and tip onto a clean, floured surface. Divide into four portions and form each one into a ball. Roll out into a 20cm diameter round using a rolling pin. Crimp up the sides to make a wall around the edge, a bit like a Chicago-style pizza. Pinch this in all the way around so that you lift up the side you have created. They should be about 15cm across with sides 2.5cm high. Carefully transfer to a baking sheet lined with oiled baking paper. If the dough collapses a little just re-work the sides. Repeat with the remaining dough. Bake for 9–10 minutes, until the bread starts to rise.

4. Remove the breads from the oven. Using a teaspoon, push the bottom down so that the well in the middle of the bread is deep enough to hold the filling. Spoon the lamb into the centre of each bread and push it up to the sides. Crack the eggs into the middle of the lamb and season with salt and a tiny bit of allspice. Return to the oven and bake for 12–15 minutes until the egg is just set. Serve immediately.

DESSERTS & SWEETS

CAROB MOLASSES & TAHINI FRENCH TOAST

This rather decadent dessert, which, by the way, makes one hell of a sweet breakfast, uses Lebanese store-cupboard staples. It's a mum's trick when pudding has been overlooked, mixing carob molasses and tahini into a dreamy, caramel-like sauce and serving it with flatbreads for dunking. The carob tree is a rather wonderful specimen, somewhat similar in appearance to an olive tree. Its fruit is less wonderful looking – a gnarly brown pod, which is used to make the dark brown carob molasses that has an unusual, slightly acrid, taste. But mix this with tahini, and the sweetness is amplified. For my recipe, I serve this with French toast. The sauce melts over it, oozing everywhere: Sunday brunch heaven.

SERVES 2

2 eggs
60ml whole milk
½ teaspoon ground cinnamon
20g caster sugar
4 slices of brioche bread
30g butter
50g carob molasses,
    plus extra for drizzling
60g tahini, plus extra for drizzling
½ teaspoon toasted sesame
    seeds, to serve

1. Whisk the eggs with the milk, ¼ teaspoon of cinnamon and the sugar. Pour into a shallow dish and add the bread. Give both sides of the bread a really good dunk into the eggs so that they get completely covered and then leave them to stand in the dish for about 4–5 minutes turning halfway. The bread will soften quite a lot.

2. Melt half the butter in a large, non-stick frying pan over a medium heat and fry two slices of the brioche until golden. I find the first side takes about 2–3 minutes and then the second side only about 1 minute. Place on a warm serving dish and repeat to cook the remaining two slices of bread.

3. Mix the carob molasses with the tahini into a lovely, thick, dark paste. Drizzle over both slices of French toast on each plate. Scatter with the sesame seeds and remaining cinnamon. Dip a teaspoon into the molasses and then drizzle a little over both plates. Do the same with the tahini. Serve immediately.

DARK CHOCOLATE & HALVA TART

Beirut is achingly hip. You can feel the cool creativity oozing out of every brick. There are amazing independent shops, vibrant street art, banging bars, chilled-out restaurants and sophisticated clubs. Everyone knows that you can't do hipster without pared-back, industrial coffee shops with beautiful tattooed baristas and slouchy chairs. The city has many to choose from and my favourite is the Kalei Coffee Co in Mar Mikhaël. I spent lots of time in their lovely little courtyard sipping long blacks, typing up all my notes and, obviously, eating cake. They do a mean chocolate and sesame torte that was the inspiration for this recipe: a bitter dark chocolate tart offset by nutty *halva*, a sesame and sugar bar that has the texture of crumbly goat's cheese, and a wonderful sweetness.

SERVES 10–12

3 tablespoons cocoa powder
250g plain flour, plus
    extra for dusting
175g chilled butter, cubed, plus
    extra for greasing
1 egg, beaten
oil, for oiling
sea salt

For the filling
400ml double cream
70g caster sugar
300g dark (70 per cent) chocolate
150g plain halva

1. Sift the cocoa powder and flour into a mixing bowl. Add a pinch of salt and 125g of the butter. Using your fingers, work the butter into the flour to form breadcrumbs. Work in the egg and 1 tablespoon of cold water and bring together into a dough. If it looks too dry, add a few teaspoons of water. Place in an oiled mixing bowl, cover and chill for 30 minutes.

2. Butter a 23cm tart tin with sides 2.5cm deep. Tip the dough out onto a clean, lightly floured surface and roll into a circle large enough to cover the tin. Keep turning the dough so that it doesn't stick. Using your rolling pin, lift the dough over the tart tin, gently press it down into the base and push the pastry into the sides. Trim off any excess. Scrunch up some baking paper, unfold it, put it into the pastry-lined tin and fill with baking beans. Chill in the fridge for 15 minutes.

3. Preheat the oven to 200°C/180°C fan/gas mark 6. Bake the pastry for 15 minutes, then remove the beans and paper and bake for a further 5 minutes to cook the base. Remove from the oven. If the base has puffed up, gently put the beans in the baking paper back into the case and the base will deflate. Leave to cool completely in the tin. Carefully flip the pastry case out of the tin and place on a flat serving dish.

4. Meanwhile, put the remaining butter into a small pan and pour in the double cream and sugar. Heat over a low heat and cook, stirring occasionally, for 5–6 minutes until the cream is warm but not bubbling. Remove from the heat and break up the chocolate into the pan. Leave for a few minutes and then gently stir together into a glossy ganache.

5. Break up 120g of the halva into small pieces and arrange them over the bottom of the pastry case. It's nice to have a few bigger chunks for texture. Pour over the ganache and smooth it out with the back of a metal spoon. Chill in the fridge for few hours to set. Sprinkle a little sea salt over the top of the tart and top with the remaining halva. Cut into slices and serve immediately.

PUMPKIN & ROSE WATER JAZARIEH

One of my favourite souks in the world is in Tripoli, with its narrow winding streets and long covered markets. The traders are fun and really friendly, and the food is fabulous. You can find the best fresh fruit and vegetables, scented honey, fragrant rose water and all manner of spices. If you're peckish, grab a plate of crisp falafel, a juicy shawarma or bowl of creamy hummus and it will be the best you've ever eaten. On one trip, my friend Hisham took me to a tiny shop belonging to Noah Al Haddad. Noah had taken over the shop from his grandfather and they sold a very old dessert called *jazarieh*. It's slabs of pumpkin that have been cooked down for hours in a sugar syrup and then set with loads of nuts and other flavours. This home-cooked version is a little more like a sweet chutney. It's delicious on vanilla ice cream or just with a bowl of fresh fruit and a huge dollop of whipped cream.

SERVES 6–8

500g peeled, deseeded
   pumpkin, cut into wedges
½ teaspoon bicarbonate of soda
150g caster sugar
1 teaspoon rose water
juice of ½ lemon
30g walnuts, bashed into
   a rubble
20g almonds, bashed into
   a rubble

1. Put the pumpkin into a pan and cover with water. Add the bicarbonate of soda and mix well. Cover and leave to soak for 6 hours. Drain the pumpkin and rinse thoroughly. Drain again and pat dry with kitchen paper. Grate coarsely using a cheese grater.

2. Tip the sugar into a large pan and add 100ml of water, the rose water and lemon. Bring to the boil over a high heat and cook for 2–3 minutes or until the sugar has dissolved. Add the grated pumpkin and mix well. Bring to the boil, reduce the heat to medium and cook, stirring occasionally, for 15–20 minutes until the syrup has been completely absorbed into the pumpkin.

3. Cover, reduce the heat to low and cook for 50–60 minutes until the pumpkin is lovely and soft, and a little glassy looking. Remove from the heat and leave to cool. Add the walnuts and almonds, mix well and serve immediately.

PEANUT HONEYCOMB
[FISTKIEH]

Dessert shops selling ice cream, biscuits and pastries are commonplace in Lebanon. It's fair to say that the country has something of a sweet tooth. Scan the shelves and you will come across these *fistkieh*, or peanut bars, made by adding a generous amount of toasted peanuts to a sugar syrup, along with bicarbonate of soda. The bicarbonate of soda explodes in a mad rush of bubbles, creating the light honeycomb that sets around the nuts. A few shards of *fistkieh* are great with a coffee or crumbled over ice cream.

SERVES 6

175g unsalted peanuts
250g caster sugar
2 tablespoons golden syrup
2 teaspoons bicarbonate of soda
oil, for oiling

1. Preheat the oven to 200°C/180°C fan/gas mark 6 and tip the peanuts into a baking tin. Toast for 18–20 minutes, shaking the tin every 4–5 minutes, until golden. Remove from the oven and set aside.

2. Pour the sugar into a deep, heavy-based saucepan and add the golden syrup. Heat gently over a medium heat until the sugar has completely dissolved and become clear.

3. Tip the peanuts into the pan and mix together. Add the bicarbonate of soda and mix once. It will fizz up madly, which is why you need to use a deep pan. Pour into a baking dish lined with oiled baking paper. Leave to cool completely.

4. Remove the peanut honeycomb from the tin and peel off the baking paper. Smash into shards and serve immediately.

PISTACHIO & CLOTTED CREAM ICE CREAM

Right on the edge of the medina in Tripoli you will find Balha Glace, an ice-cream parlour famous for *ashta* and pistachio ice cream. Traditional *ashta* is clotted cream and is used as the base of many Lebanese desserts. Here it gives the ice cream a really wonderful texture. The old boys who run the dessert parlour fill a Mr Whippy-style cone with *ashta* ice cream and then dunk the top into a tray of smashed pistachios that stick all over it. The consistency of clotted cream makes this a really good no-churn ice cream, so an ice-cream maker isn't essential. It stays velvety and doesn't crystallise. To get the right colour for my *ashta* ice cream, the crazy-green Iranian pistachios are best, and then you can use normal kernels for the coating. If you can't find the Iranian variety, just blitz up any non-salted kernels you can find.

SERVES 6

100g slivered Iranian pistachios
150g caster sugar
250ml whole milk
2 eggs, whisked
250ml double cream
227g tub clotted cream
50g pistachio kernels,
    bashed into a fine rubble

1. Put the Iranian pistachios into a food-processor with 110g of the sugar. Blend for a few minutes until really fine. Tip into a saucepan and add the milk. Bring to the boil, stirring occasionally, over a low heat.

2. Whisk the eggs with the remaining sugar in a large mixing bowl until fluffy and pale. Gradually whisk in the milk mixture. Return to the pan and reheat over a low heat, whisking continuously, for 10–12 minutes or until the custard is really thick. Pour into a dish and leave to cool completely. Cover with clingfilm and chill in the fridge for 2 hours.

3. Pour the double cream into a large mixing bowl and whisk into soft peaks. Fold in the clotted cream and then the chilled custard. Make sure it is mixed together thoroughly and evenly.

4. Churn in an ice-cream maker, then transfer to the freezer. If you don't have an ice-cream maker, pour the mixture into a freezerproof container. Freeze for 2 hours, remove and then whisk together with a fork. Return to the freezer and repeat after 2 hours. Then leave to freeze for 4–6 hours until set.

5. Remove the ice cream from the freezer about 10 minutes before you want to eat. Tip the pistachio kernels into a shallow dish. Dip an ice-cream scoop into hot water and scoop out balls of the ice cream. Tip into the pistachios and roll them around so that they are completely covered in the green nuts. Transfer to serving bowls and serve immediately.

LEBANESE NIGHTS DESSERT

[LAYALI LUBNAN]

I came across this particular dessert in the little village of Ramliyeh in the Chouf Mountains. My friend Rima had prepared a stomach-stretching feast for me, culminating in these creamy little pudding pots called Lebanese Nights Dessert. What a killer name! It's almost heroic. The pud itself is one of those typically Arabic desserts made with sweet semolina cream, set in the fridge and then topped with whipped cream. Its soft texture and sweet taste is as pleasing as a similarly mushy pudding I remember from my childhood – Angel Delight. I was hooked on Rima's dessert. For my version, I have strayed from her recipe by using rose water, lemon and dried apricots to give it more of a luxurious finish.

SERVES 4

250ml whole milk
50g fine semolina
70g condensed milk
1 tablespoon plus
　½ teaspoon rose water
zest and juice of ½ lemon
200ml double cream
2 tablespoons icing sugar

To decorate
4 dried apricots, thinly sliced
5g toasted flaked almonds
1 tablespoon dried rose petals

1. Pour the milk into a non-stick saucepan and tip in the semolina. Whisk together over a low heat for 8–10 minutes until lovely and thick. Add the condensed milk, the tablespoon of rose water and the lemon zest. Whisk together. Remove from the heat and leave to cool for 2–3 minutes. Pour into four tall serving glasses and chill in the fridge for 15–20 minutes.

2. Meanwhile, whisk the double cream with the lemon juice, icing sugar and remaining rose water into luscious soft peaks. Spoon the mixture over the top of the glasses and pop them back in the fridge to chill for a further 15–20 minutes. You can make these the day before and leave them like this very happily in the fridge overnight. Top the puddings with slices of apricot and a few flaked almonds. Scatter over the rose petals and serve immediately.

DULCE DE LECHE KNAFEH

Knafeh is a very old Arabic dessert. Explaining the dish is a hard sell. I mean, fried noodle-like pastry stuffed with cheese and cooked in sugar syrup sounds strange. But think about it: crisp buttery pastry filled with oozy cheese (there for its textural delight, not flavour) to soak up a sweet syrup ... well, now we've gone somewhere interesting. The basis of my recipe is very traditional, but I couldn't help riffing on it a little and updating it with a drizzle of smoky dulce de leche and a scoop of vanilla ice cream. I always try to make my recipes inclusive, but the pastry for knafeh is very specific and one you have to buy from a Middle Eastern store. The thin strands of pastry are super-fine vermicelli and give the finished knafeh the most amazing crunch.

SERVES 4

30g caster sugar
1 teaspoon rose water
1 teaspoon lemon juice
160g knafeh pastry
65g butter
65g mozzarella
60g dulce de leche

To serve
vanilla ice cream
slivered Iranian pistachios,
    bashed into a fine rubble

1. Put the caster sugar, rose water, lemon juice and 80ml water into a small saucepan and bring to the boil over a high heat. Cook for a few minutes until clear. Remove from the heat and set aside.

2. Separate out the knafeh pastry into a mixing bowl. Don't break it up too much. You want lovely long strands of the pastry.

3. Melt 55g of the butter in a small saucepan over a low heat and pour over the knafeh pastry. Mix well so that the strands are completely covered in butter.

4. Melt 5g of butter in a small, non-stick frying pan over a low–medium heat. Add half the pastry and push it out to form a small round (about 10cm diameter). Top with the cheese, leaving about a 1cm border of pastry around the cheese. Add the remaining pastry and spread out over the cheese so it's the same thickness as the bottom layer. Use a spoon to pull in the sides to make them neat and gently push down the top so that it's even. Cook for 4–6 minutes until golden on the bottom.

5. Carefully flip the knafeh out of the pan onto a plate. Melt the remaining butter in the pan and slide the knafeh back in. Use the spoon to tidy up the edges. Cook for 3–4 minutes until crisp and golden on the bottom.

6. Increase the heat to high and pour over the sugar syrup. It will bubble quite fiercely so watch out. Cook for 1–2 minutes until it's all absorbed and then flip the knafeh out onto a serving plate.

7. Meanwhile, heat the dulce de leche in a small pan over a low heat. As it warms it will loosen up.

8. To serve, top the knafeh with a few scoops of ice cream. Drizzle over the dulce de leche, scatter over the pistachios and serve immediately.

DATE & CINNAMON SQUARES

[MAAMOUL MAD]

Maamoul mad is a crumbly semolina pastry, baked in layers with a date filling. Abu Hassan has been making it in a shady stone archway in the souks of Saida, or Sidon, for years. Every day he makes vast round trays of *maamoul mad*, getting the top beautifully golden and crispy without ever burning the sides. Once cooked, he cuts the vast pastry into little squares and ships them all over Lebanon. His version is the best. Sadly, despite my most charming efforts, Abu just roared with laughter every time I asked for the recipe. So this is my version, covered in runny honey and a fine rubble of nuts. And it's just as good. Look for *mahlab* in a Middle Eastern store. It's a spice made from the ground stones of a cherry, and is a traditional spice for making dessert pastry in Lebanon.

SERVES 15–20

225g semolina
110g fine semolina
130g caster sugar
3.5g (½ sachet) fast-action yeast
½ teaspoon mahlab (optional)
4 tablespoons rose water
170g butter, melted,
    plus extra for greasing
95g walnuts
500g Medjool dates, pitted and
    any bits of stalk removed
½ teaspoon ground cinnamon
4 tablespoons runny honey
25g pistachio kernels, bashed
    into a rubble

1. Tip the two types of semolina into a mixing bowl and add the caster sugar, yeast and mahlab (if using). Mix well. Add 2 tablespoons of the rose water and the melted butter. Mix together and then rub the semolina between the palms of your hands to separate out the grains as much as possible. Cover and chill in the fridge for 2 hours.

2. Meanwhile, put the walnuts in a food-processor and blitz until fine. Set aside 25g. Add the dates to the food-processor along with the remaining rose water and the cinnamon. Blitz together into a paste.

3. Butter a 23cm round cake tin. Take the semolina out of the fridge and quickly work the mixture with your hands to separate out the grains again. Tip half into the cake tin. Spread out evenly, then press down with the palm of your hand to form a solid base.

4. Next you want a layer of the date mixture. It's easiest to do this in stages. Wet your hands to stop the dates from sticking ,then take a small piece of the date mixture and flatten it out. Put it into the tin and then continue until you have a layer covering the semolina. Wet your hands again and smooth the dates out into an even layer.

5. Preheat the oven to 200°C/180°C fan/gas mark 6. Top the date layer with the remaining semolina. Even out and then press down firmly to form an even layer. Run a sharp knife around the edge of the tin. Bake for 30–35 minutes until golden. Remove and leave to cool completely.

6. Cover the cake tin with a large plate and carefully invert the maamoul mad to release it from the tin. Then cover it with a serving plate and flip again so that the lovely golden side is on top. Drizzle over the honey, then scatter the pistachios and remaining walnuts over the top. Cut into little squares and serve immediately.

LEBANESE CANNOLI
[ZNOUD EL SIT]

Traditionally made as a sweet treat for Iftar, the evening meal that ends the daily fast during Ramadan, these wonderful little pastries are stuffed with creamy *ashta*, a thick blend of sweet semolina and milk, and deep fried until crisp. You can make them at home or grab them in a café to have as an accompaniment to coffee. *Znoud el sit* means 'ladies' upper arms' in reference, I was told, to the delicate texture and shape. I'd like to think it's because of the enviable golden tan and taut finish. These cannoli are wonderful anytime, and to make a decadent dessert, I finish mine off with honey, rose petals and pistachios.

MAKES 12 / SERVES 4

50g butter
250ml whole milk,
   plus extra for brushing
60g fine semolina
2 tablespoons caster sugar
1 teaspoon rose water
6 sheets filo pastry
vegetable oil, for deep-frying
4 tablespoons runny honey

To *garnish*
1 teaspoon rose petals
15g slivered Iranian pistachios

1. Melt the butter in a pan over a medium heat. Pour in the milk and add the semolina, sugar and rose water. Whisk together for 3–4 minutes until lovely and thick. Tip into a shallow, rectangular dish, cover and refrigerate for a few hours until completely chilled. With a knife, score into twelve portions.

2. Take a sheet of filo pastry and place it on a chopping board so it's landscape to you. Cut it in half horizontally into two rectangles. Lay out both pieces so they are portrait to you.

3. Take a portion of the filling and spread it out into a little sausage shape 4–5cm long at the bottom end of one of the filo pastry strips. Start to roll it up tightly. After a few turns, tuck in the sides and continue to roll up into a neat cigar shape. Place onto a plate lined with clingfilm and cover. Repeat with the rest and put into the fridge to chill for 5 minutes.

4. Heat the vegetable oil in a saucepan over a medium-high heat. You need about 7–10cm of oil – enough to completely cover the znoud. To see if the oil is hot enough, drop in a tiny piece of filo pastry. It should bubble up to the surface immediately. Fry 2–3 znoub at a time for about 1–1½ minutes until golden. Remove with a slotted spoon and drain on kitchen paper for a few seconds. Transfer to a serving plate and repeat with the rest. Drizzle with the honey and garnish with rose petals and pistachios. Serve immediately.

ROSE WATER & PISTACHIO CHEESECAKE

My sensational cheesecake is inspired by various Lebanese desserts called *madlouka*, which means 'to pour' in Arabic. The *madlouka* in question had a round, crumbly semolina base that was spread out over a plate and topped with pillowy soft cream and loads of nuts. In my head it had a cheesecake format already. Rather than using semolina, I have used a traditional biscuit base and added ground pistachios for added oomph. The lusciously light topping is a mix of cream cheese and clotted cream, perfumed with rose water. Simplicity at its best.

SERVES 8–10

For the base
70g pistachio kernels
200g digestive biscuits
100g butter, melted,
   plus extra for greasing
2 tablespoons rose water
1 teaspoon mahlab
   (optional; see page 183)

For the topping
227g tub of clotted cream
400g cream cheese
100g icing sugar
1 tablespoon rose water

To decorate
10g slivered Iranian pistachios,
   bashed until fine
1 tablespoon dried rose petals

1. To make the base, put the pistachios into a food-processor and blend until fine. Add the biscuits and continue to blend until fine. Pour in the melted butter, rose water and mahlab, if using. Blend together.

2. Grease and line a 25cm spring-form cake tin with baking paper. Tip the biscuit base into the tin and spread out evenly. Press down with your hands to pack it together and form a solid base. Put into the fridge to chill for 30 minutes.

3. Meanwhile, scoop the clotted cream into a mixing bowl and whisk into soft peaks.

4. Put the cream cheese into a separate mixing bowl, add the icing sugar and mix until smooth. Scrape into the bowl with the clotted cream and pour in the rose water. Whisk together into firm peaks. Spoon in an even layer over the cheesecake base. Return it to the fridge and chill for 2 hours until firm.

5. Take the cheesecake out of the fridge and remove it from the tin. Slide the cheesecake onto a serving plate or board. Peel off the paper from the sides and garnish with the pistachios and rose petals. Serve immediately.

INDEX

ACKNOWLEDGEMENTS

Saffron in the Souks has been a wondrous book for me to write. A real adventure and I have loved getting stuck in. From beginning to end I have had the support of Kamal Mouzawak. You helped unlock the land and introduced me to the best home cooks in the world. A million thank yous. I want to give a special mention to Fadia Chaptini in Jounieh; Georgina Bayeh in Zhgarta – I loved your *kibbeh*; Rita Ezhaya in Jezzine; Rima Massoud who taught me all about Druze food; Chef Dima Al Chaar for being generally badass; Rima Khodr in Beirut; Jonny and the whole team at Beit Ammiq; and Rima Husseini at the Palmyra hotel in Baalbek. And an extended round of applause to everyone at Souk El Tayeb.

Also a shout out to Bethany Kehdy, a gorgeous creature and talented food writer who has been so helpful and introduced me to Hisham Assaad, my favourite foodie guide and drinking buddy, through her company Taste Lebanon.

Closer to home, fist pumps to my wonderful editor Tara, I love working with you. She makes me look proper polished and has become a pro at dealing with me – spoiler alert, I might be a tiny bit of a mega control freak. Judith, thanks for doing another book with me, here's to many more. And everyone at Kyle Books, Victoria Scales that's you too, thank you for making it as seamless as always. Dr Lise Storm, you fact check my work wonderfully – thank you. Anna, Geraldine and Kate, my lovely agents at Yellow Poppy Media, your support is invaluable.

Last but not least, my glam squad. Nassima Rothacker, darl you are the most talented photographer in town. Rosie Reynolds, you win the prize for the best food stylist ever. Nine months pregnant and you worked harder than all of us. Wei Tang, who has done all of my books and nailed each one, babe what a triumph you are. The flowers were genius. Smith & Gilmour, you have put together an incredible book. And finally Alan Keohane, who makes the travel side of my books come to life so beautifully; quite simply Al, I couldn't do it without you.

Finally to my wonderful family who are the most important people to me on the planet; Sal and Al, especially you two. I bloody love you both. And, yes, Rosie and Tom – my way older siblings – that includes both of you, so no squabbling this time. This also extends, of course, to Giles and Rachel, and all the kids; Daisy, Jake, Finn, Dylan and Anya (keep being wonderful and entertaining your uncle so well) – and all my brilliantly bonkers extended family. Love you all!